the
SERMON
on the
MOUNT

TEACHINGS FROM MATTHEW 6

WRITTEN BY
PASTOR JOHN CARTER &
PASTOR CHUCK LINDSEY

DESIGNED BY LORENA HABER
FORMATTED BY SHAWNA JOHNSON
EDITED BY DR. RANDY T. JOHNSON & JEANNIE YATES

THE RIVER CHURCH
REACH | GATHER | GROW

CONTENTS

PREFACE

What is life about?
What should my life goals be?
How do I pray?
What is fasting?
What do I do with money?
What do I do about anxiety?
What's the right way to give?

These are just a few of the questions answered by the Lord Jesus in the sixth chapter of Matthew's Gospel. You may have asked these questions and you may be asking them today.

The words of this chapter fall directly in the middle of the most famous of Jesus' sermons called the "Sermon on the Mount." In this great sermon, the Lord Jesus is speaking to a multitude of normal people. It was people like you and me. They were married, unmarried, raising kids, empty nesters, grandparents, aunts, uncles, employed, unemployed, homemakers, home-owners, homeless, healthy, ill, known, unknown, Jewish, Gentile, male, female, adult, and children. He speaks in common language using common pictures to help common people understand eternal truths.

In *"The Sermon on the Mount,"* we will try to place ourselves there, on that grassy hillside in Galilee, among the crowd to not only listen to Him speak but to be changed by His words. Our goal will be to come away from this book the way many came away from the sermon that day - changed forever.

"The Sermon on the Mount" contains nine study guides for group discussion and fifty-four devotions for personal development. The goal of *"The Sermon on the Mount"* is for the reader first to realize their sinful condition and need for a Savior. Once that is settled, we need to live for the Lord. It is not always easy. Jesus addresses some very challenging topics. With Him, you can take on the challenge.

MATTHEW SIX

[1] *"Beware of practicing your righteousness before other people in order to be seen by them, for then you will have no reward from your Father who is in heaven.*

[2] *"Thus, when you give to the needy, sound no trumpet before you, as the hypocrites do in the synagogues and in the streets, that they may be praised by others. Truly, I say to you, they have received their reward.* [3] *But when you give to the needy, do not let your left hand know what your right hand is doing,* [4] *so that your giving may be in secret. And your Father who sees in secret will reward you.*

[5] *"And when you pray, you must not be like the hypocrites. For they love to stand and pray in the synagogues and at the street corners, that they may be seen by others. Truly, I say to you, they have received their reward.* [6] *But when you pray, go into your room and shut the door and pray to your Father who is in secret. And your Father who sees in secret will reward you.*

[7] *"And when you pray, do not heap up empty phrases as the Gentiles do, for they think that they will be heard for their many words.* [8] *Do not be like them, for your Father knows what you need before you ask him.* [9] *Pray then like this:*

"Our Father in heaven,
hallowed be your name.
[10] *Your kingdom come,*
your will be done,
 on earth as it is in heaven.
[11] *Give us this day our daily bread,*
[12] *and forgive us our debts,*
 as we also have forgiven our debtors.
[13] *And lead us not into temptation,*
 but deliver us from evil.

14 For if you forgive others their trespasses, your heavenly Father will also forgive you, 15 but if you do not forgive others their trespasses, neither will your Father forgive your trespasses.

16 "And when you fast, do not look gloomy like the hypocrites, for they disfigure their faces that their fasting may be seen by others. Truly, I say to you, they have received their reward. 17 But when you fast, anoint your head and wash your face, 18 that your fasting may not be seen by others but by your Father who is in secret. And your Father who sees in secret will reward you.

19 "Do not lay up for yourselves treasures on earth, where moth and rust destroy and where thieves break in and steal, 20 but lay up for yourselves treasures in heaven, where neither moth nor rust destroys and where thieves do not break in and steal. 21 For where your treasure is, there your heart will be also.

22 "The eye is the lamp of the body. So, if your eye is healthy, your whole body will be full of light, 23 but if your eye is bad, your whole body will be full of darkness. If then the light in you is darkness, how great is the darkness!

24 "No one can serve two masters, for either he will hate the one and love the other, or he will be devoted to the one and despise the other. You cannot serve God and money.

25 "Therefore I tell you, do not be anxious about your life, what you will eat or what you will drink, nor about your body, what you will put on. Is not life more than food, and the body more than clothing? 26 Look at the birds of the air: they neither sow nor reap nor gather into barns, and yet your heavenly Father feeds them. Are you not of more value than they? 27 And which of you by being anxious can add a single hour to his span of life? 28 And why are you anxious about clothing? Consider the lilies of the field, how they grow: they neither

toil nor spin, ²⁹ yet I tell you, even Solomon in all his glory
was not arrayed like one of these. ³⁰ But if God so clothes
the grass of the field, which today is alive and tomorrow is
thrown into the oven, will he not much more clothe you, O
you of little faith?³¹ Therefore do not be anxious, saying, 'What
shall we eat?' or 'What shall we drink?' or 'What shall we
wear?' ³² For the Gentiles seek after all these things, and your
heavenly Father knows that you need them all. ³³ But seek
first the kingdom of God and his righteousness, and all these
things will be added to you."

LESSON ONE

Giving to Those in Need

PASTOR CHUCK LINDSEY

The New Testament of the Bible was written entirely in Greek. The original letters and books of the New Testament were all originally penned in the common language of the day; Koine Greek. The authors of the New Testament all spoke and wrote in it and our English New Testament Bibles have all been translated from it.

I love the Greek language, I really do. I love its precision. I love its nuances. I love its clarity. As a pastor, I have been studying it now for over 20 years. That said, I do not, by any stretch, profess to be a Greek language scholar. There are men and women who have devoted their entire lives to the study of that language. I am not one of them. I study Greek (or Hebrew for the Old Testament) for the purpose of understanding the original intent and meaning of the original writers. I want to know exactly what they were trying to say at the time that they said it. That is what I am after.

The Greek language is a language of precision (unlike English!). An example of the difference between Greek and English can be found in the word "love." In English, we use the word "love" to express our love for ice cream and our love for our children. However, the love that we are speaking about is not the same for each. The love I have for my children is infinitely beyond the love I have for ice cream (although pumpkin ice cream gets close). By contrast, in Greek, there are four separate words for "love":

- The Greek word **"phileo"** describes a deep brotherly love.
- The Greek word **"storge"** describes familial love.
- The Greek word **"eros"** describes intimate or sexual love.
- The Greek word **"agape"** describes a divine, supernatural love.

This precision is carried further by the fact that its language centers around its verbs. In Greek, the text is carried along by its verbs. In short, verbs are a big deal in the Greek language.

1. Have you studied any foreign languages?

_____

_____

_____

2. Do you have any examples of that language being translated differently into English?

_____

_____

_____

I tell you this because, as we move through Matthew chapter 6, we are going to emphasize key Greek words, specifically the verbs that Jesus uses to say what He wants to say. We will highlight them. So, all Greek verbs will be underlined and in **bold** (like this). Some Greek nouns will be emphasized as well. Our focus will be on the verbs as they are the key to unlocking and understanding the passage.

One last thing to mention before we dive in, as we come to the words of Jesus in Matthew chapter 6, is that we are not entering into a new thing. What I mean is, chapter 6 is actually smacked in the middle of Jesus' famous "Sermon on the Mount" which was given to the multitudes. It began in chapter 5 and stretches into chapter 7.

I have been to this mountain teaching spot in Israel. It is quite a sight. The mount is a large hillside with a natural bowl-like curve and slope. It could easily seat five thousand or more people, and because of its shape and size it is an ideal amphitheater. I was amazed to be able to hear clearly the words of someone speaking at the bottom from the top. Jesus chose His spot well.

That said, we have come into the middle of this master of all sermons.

Giving to Those in Need

Matthew 6:1-4 (NKJV) says, ***"Take heed that you do not do your charitable deeds before men, to be seen by them. Otherwise*** *you have no reward from your Father in heaven. Therefore, when you do a charitable deed, do not sound a trumpet before you as the hypocrites do in the synagogues and in the streets, that they may have glory from men. Assuredly, I say to you, they have their reward. But when you do a charitable deed, do not let your left hand know what your right hand is doing, that your charitable deed may be in secret; and your Father who sees in secret will Himself reward you openly."*

I want to first look at Matthew 6:1 (NKJV), *"Take heed that you do not do your charitable deeds before men, to be seen by them. Otherwise you have no reward from your Father in heaven."*

Chapter 6 begins with a warning that repeats several times throughout Matthew's Gospel. The Lord Jesus tells us to *"**take heed**."* *"**Take heed**"* comes from the Greek verb "Prosecho" and means "to hold in mind."

It was a nautical term that meant to hold a ship in a certain direction to avoid drifting off course. In this instance, our Lord is using it in the negative. He is telling us to avoid, steer clear of, or away from something. If we continue the boat analogy, then there is an iceberg in the water that we must be careful to avoid! To *"**Take heed**"* is to watch carefully for a very real danger.

    3.   What are some "icebergs" that we need to avoid?

<u>Satans Lies, Distractions</u>

_____

_____

He tells us that we must be careful with what we *"**do**."* *"**Do**"* comes from the Greek verb "Poieo" and means "to be (busy) about."

The emphasis here is not just on *what* we do but on *how* we do what we do. The warning is in relation to our *"charitable deeds,"* which refers to any way that we would help others who are in need. Our King tells us to be careful *how* we help others.

His instruction is to be careful when we **"_do_"** these things, that we do not do them "to be **seen**." "To be **seen**" comes from the Greek verb "Theaomai" and means "to stare at or to look intently at something."

Jesus is warning us against doing the right things in the wrong ways. Specifically, we are not to do them in a way that causes people to concentrate or focus on us. He said something similar when He said, **"Let your light so shine before men, that they may see your good works and glorify your Father in heaven"** (Matthew 5:16, NKJV).

4. How do we sometimes do the right thing in the wrong way?

Tell others what we have done

Everyone listening to Jesus' warning here knew what He was referring to. It was not uncommon in that day to see religious leaders (Sadducees, Scribes, and Pharisees) come into the temple with an entourage of people blowing trumpets, making noise, and calling attention to themselves. As soon as all eyes were on them, the religious leader would piously step forward to drop his offering into the box for all to see (and admire!). Jesus was revealing that the goal of those who give like this is not to help the poor or needy but rather to be admired by others. Do not do this! Jesus says, "Steer your boat in the opposite direction of what you have seen them do." The goal in giving must always be to help those in need and honor the Lord. It must never be to promote ourselves.

At the end of verse one, we are confronted with a choice. It is found in the word **"_have_."** **"_Have_"** comes from the Greek verb "Echo" and means "to have or hold."

Jesus tells us that we can **"_have_"** one of only two rewards. The first is what He has already said, **"to be seen by"** people. This **"reward"** is that people will see us, see what we have done, and admire us. Insert sarcasm: What a reward! The second **"reward"** is from our **"Father in heaven"** and it is His seeing. He sees what we have done and it brings Him joy. The reward is His approval.

The whole of the New Testament teaches that the reward of Heaven is not gold or physical treasures but rather, His happiness with us. One day, He will say to each of us, **"Well done, good and faithful servant; you were faithful over a few things, I will make you ruler over many things. Enter into the joy of your Lord"** (Matthew 25:21, NKJV). It is this, His approval of us, that will be the great reward of Heaven. Jesus tells us to choose between the momentary admiration of people or the eternal approval of our King. He says that it is one or the other and that we forfeit the one to gain the other. The choice seems obvious!

Steer clear of doing good things to be admired by people. For in so doing, you give up the eternal reward from your Father.

Matthew 6:2 (NKJV) continues, **"Therefore, when you do a charitable deed, do not sound a trumpet before you as the hypocrites do in the synagogues and in the streets, that they may have glory from men. Assuredly, I say to you, they have their reward."**

Verse two begins with, what would have been to His audience, a familiar illustration. We have mentioned it already. He calls attention to the "giving" practice of religious leaders. He calls them **"hypocrites."**

"Hypocrites" comes from the Greek verb hupokrites and means "to play a part, to act, to pretend."

It comes from a word that means to "wear a mask" and described actors in a play who would change masks to change characters in the play. Jesus calls these religious leaders "mask-wearers" and "actors." He is telling us that what they *were* doing and what they *appeared to be* doing were two different things. They appeared to be giving to the needs of others. This was an act. The reality is that they were giving to be praised by others.

5. In what ways do people wear masks today?

_Church face, pretend all is ok,
over active in church activities for
recognition, Act one way but heart is another_

Jesus sets the contrast between what we **"_do_"** and what they **"_do._"** They **"_sound a trumpet_"** before they give so that they are seen and admired. Their goal, Jesus says is **"_glory_ from men."** **"Glory"** comes from the Greek word "Doxa" and means "to recognize a person or thing for what they are".

In terms of religious leaders, they are wanting people to recognize them as great men, generous men, and morally above others. They want human recognition and honor and do not care about God's recognition or the needs of others. They were pretenders. They were like Judas whose objection to the perfumed offering was false. He exclaimed that "it could have been sold and the money given to the poor" but we read that he said this **"_not that he cared for the poor, but because he was a thief, and had the money box; and he used to take what was put in it"_** (John 12:6, NKJV). He was an actor. He had ulterior motives. Here Jesus says, they **"_have_"** what they are actually seeking; the approval of people. They will not have any honor or recognition from the Lord. They have made their choice, and they chose poorly.

When you help someone else, do not call attention to it. The recognition that comes from people is a poor reward.

Matthew 6:3 (NKJV) adds, **"_But when you do a charitable deed, do not let your left hand know what your right hand is doing."_**

6. What does Jesus mean here concerning one's hands?

_no need to let others know, Don't
make a big deal out of it, be
humble._

As we come into verse three the emphasis is on intentional ignorance. Ignorance? Yes. Jesus tells us that when we **_"do"_** something to meet the needs of another person, we are to, in some sense, ignore what we have done. He tells us not to let our left hand **_"know"_** what our right hand has done. It is a funny picture, but in simple terms, this means that we are not to make a big deal out of what we have done. We **_"do"_** it and move on. It is a warning against calling attention to it, working to get others to see it, know it, and appreciate it. He is telling us not to wait for praise or congratulations.

He will tell us in verse four to do it in **_"secret."_** Others should be ignorant of what we have given or done. Giving is done correctly when God moves us to give, we move into action, and then we move on!

When you help someone else, do not make a big deal out of it. Just do it for the glory of God and for the good of the other person.

Matthew 6:4 (NKJV) records, **_"That your charitable deed may be in secret; and your Father who sees in secret will Himself reward you openly."_**

7. Have you ever experienced someone paying it forward? What were your thoughts? How did it feel?

> That has been a slogan of mine - to pay it forward. You may never recieve back from whom you helped, but from some one else!

8. What are some good things we can do in secret?

> We have to first be alert - to our surroundings - There are times we help strangers - a few times bought gas for people -

Finally, our Lord tells us what will happen if we choose to give in this way. He says that we will be rewarded. Verse four begins with the phrase **_"so that"_** and it means "give like this so that this will happen." He is reminding you and me of something. Our *"Father"* *"**sees**"* everything - every single thing. He *"**sees**."*

"Sees" comes from the Greek verb "Blepo" and means to look at, to watch. He *"**sees**"* what is done, when no one else *"**sees**"* what is done. He knows what is given when no one else knows what is given. *"Your Father"* *"**sees**"* what is done in *"secret."*

"Secret" comes from the Greek word "Kruptos" and means "concealed, hidden." The promise is that He will (one day) *"reward you openly."* *"**Reward**"* comes from the Greek word "Apodidomi" and means "to give from."

This word is a combination of two Greek words. The first means "to give" the second means "from" and so the word *"**reward**"* means that our Lord will give to us from His treasures. There are amazing treasures in His storehouses! Just think of what He, who is limitless in His resources and ability, is able to give to you whom He loves. Just think of how He is supremely able to bless you. In 1 Corinthians 2:9 (NKJV), we read, *"Eye has not seen, nor ear heard, nor have entered into the heart of man the things which God has prepared for those who love Him."* You and I cannot even imagine the blessings of His rewards to us. They infinitely surpass any human recognition or congratulations. Jesus says this to assure us, that we do not need to seek human reward for our *"Father who sees in secret will Himself reward you openly."*

One final point needs to be made here. The tense of the verb *"**reward**"* is future. This means that His *"**reward**"* is not here and now, on this Earth. The *"**reward**"* is in the future. The *"**reward**"* is coming. The *"**reward**"* will be given one day, a great day, the day of His *"**reward**."* Try to imagine for even a moment what it will be like for Him to reward you!

9. What kinds of rewards have you received?

I think of "rewards" as blessings-

10. What do you think about when you hear of God's rewards?

Blessings

Please notice that it will not be an angel or a messenger who rewards you. It is He **"Himself"** who will **"_reward_"** you. Notice also that His reward will not then be in **"secret."** He will **"reward you openly"** a phrase that means "for all to see." If this does not convince us to choose His **reward** over the recognition of people, I do not know what could. **"His reward is with Him"** (Isaiah 40:10, NKJV).

What you have done in secret is seen by Him who sees all. He is your Father and on that day, He will pour out His limitless blessing to bless you.

NOTES

CHARITY

DEVOTION #1 - PASTOR JOHN CARTER

As we walk through this series and focus particularly on the passages of Matthew chapter 6, I wanted to give you some real and practical ways to read these devotions. These devotions will walk day-by-day through the particular passage we are studying. Sometimes it might just be a phrase or word that really sticks out or leads us to the power and substance of God's Word. I intentionally made them short so they would quickly point you to the meat of the subject.

This week, we are going to walk through Jesus' teaching on charity, or giving. Jesus, over the next several weeks, is going to walk us through the comparison and contrast of the right way to give versus the wrong way to give. You often hear this in church, "Just tell me the right way; I can figure out the wrong stuff." Churches in the past have been ridiculed for always only pointing out the "what not to do" with very few instructions on "what to do." Jesus is going to give us plenty of both. If we do not take an honest approach to the things God says "not" to do then we may very well find ourselves in the traps and lies of the devil. I am very thankful that Jesus gives us both so that we can not only see the warning and what to be careful of but He also instructs us in the proper way to walk.

This week we are going to walk through the subject of giving, or charity. Before we really dive into Matthew chapter 6, I think the following passage is a good reminder for us. As Kind David opened the assembly at the temple in prayer, he pointed to some powerful truths.

In 1 Chronicles 29:10-13, we read, **"Therefore David blessed the Lord in the presence of all the assembly. And David said: 'Blessed are you, O Lord, the God of Israel our father, forever and ever. Yours, O Lord, is the greatness and the power and** *the glory and the victory and the majesty, for all that is in the heavens and in the earth is yours. Yours is the kingdom, O Lord, and you are exalted as head above all. Both riches and honor come from you, and you rule over all. In your hand are power and might, and in your hand it is to make great and to give strength to all. And now we thank you, our God, and praise your glorious name.'"*

David, with all of the victories in battle, wealth, power, and security they received, recognizes that it all came by the hands of God. God blessed David and the people of Israel in many ways. David wants us to remember Who it is that actually gives us strength, power, wealth, and security. He said, *"All that is in heaven and in the earth is yours [God's]."* This is really the fundamental question we have to answer, "Do I believe that statement?" As we walk through Matthew chapter 6, we will see the comparison and contrast of those who give only to be seen versus those who give in secret.

Practically, walk through today and evaluate that question. Take time to really digest it. "Do I believe that God is in charge of all that is in Heaven and Earth?" Maybe you should ask yourself how you might act differently if you say "yes" to that question. Pray that God will show you some amazing truth from His Word this week as we dive into Jesus teaching us practical applications concerning life.

TO BE SEEN

DEVOTION #2 - PASTOR JOHN CARTER

"Beware of practicing your righteousness before other people in order to be seen by them, for then you will have no reward from your Father who is in heaven." Matthew 6:1

If you have kids, or even young nieces or nephews, you can probably relate to the idea of how excited they get when they want to share something amazing they have done. It might be that they colored between the lines for the first time, so they are bringing a picture for you to see. They may want to show you they were able to achieve a new Karate move in their Karate class, so they demonstrate it for you. If you spend just a short period of time with children, it will be inevitable that in some form or fashion the child will want to show you something to receive your praise or recognition. Kids are always looking for the opportunity to get the approval of their parents, so they continually bring things to us as parents that they think we will be proud of or pleased with. Similar to kids, we (as adults) like people to know the good things or the amazing things we do in order to be recognized. In other words, we like to be seen.

We see this idea of being seen played out in many different factors of our adult lives. As young adults, we like to recognize the best and brightest students. We have bumper stickers put on the back of cars that talk about how smart our kids are. In the workplace, we strive to be recognized for our good work, and maybe our good ideas that help the place of employment we are at. More than anywhere else, we really see this idea of being seen on social media outlets. Sometimes as you are scrolling through these social media platforms, you see people's good posts and it gives you warm and fuzzy feel-good emotions. Ultimately, we all want to be seen and recognized for the things we do or the amazing accomplishments we participate in.

So, why does Jesus warn us when it comes to the practicing of our righteousness (which is an amazing accomplishment) to not do it to be seen by others? Should we not be an example for the world? The major aspect of this text and the best way to understand it is in the title, "To Be Seen." *Pride, focus off Christ*

Is our motive in being seen pointing the people to see us, or is it pointing them to Someone else? This is the battle of humanity since the beginning. We are such a prideful and boastful creation. We like the spotlight on us so we are often looking for that recognition because we want the pride of self to shine bright. We are often willing to substitute the light of ourselves to shine brighter than the glory of God.

As we walk through this week and examine some of the things Jesus is teaching us in Matthew 6:1-4, we should start by examining our own self, our motive in doing good, or practicing righteousness. Is it an authentic motive to show people about Jesus? Is it to show others His goodness? Are we wanting to share with others His rich blessings? Can you be honest with yourself and confess that maybe there have been times you have been motivated by the temporary good feeling of being seen by others? If your reward is to be seen by others, then Jesus tells us there is no reward from the Father in Heaven. If you ask me, I would much rather have an eternal reward from the Father in Heaven than a temporary reward that only lasts for the short moments of recognition.

TO BE UNSEEN

DEVOTION #3 - PASTOR JOHN CARTER

"But when you give to the needy, do not let your left hand know what your right hand is doing." Matthew 6:3

Yesterday's devotion talked about the idea of "being seen" versus today's devotion about the "unseen." If you did not read yesterday's devotion, can I encourage you to turn the page back and read it before you continue? These devotions are designed to build upon each other. As we look through this topic of secret or unseen gifts, we have to consider the contrasting difference from being seen.

Now, if you are a logical and analytical person like I am, you immediately read this verse and say, "Not possible!" There is no physical way that your left hand can do something without your right hand knowing about it. So, what is this all about? How do we make sense of what Jesus is stating here?

I am glad you see this as a physical impossibility; it means you are a rational human being. If you do not believe me, try to do something with your right hand without letting your left hand know about it. Have fun!

As I thought about this passage, another passage came to mind regarding the body. Paul uses the analogy of the body to describe the Church. The role of each member of the body is that we are all unified in mission and purpose. He ultimately says that the head of the body (or Church) is Christ. In 1 Corinthians 12:27, we read, *"Now you are the body of Christ and individually members of it."*

When you examine the statement Jesus makes in Matthew 6:3 along with what Paul teaches us, you can actually begin to see how this works. In Matthew, Jesus is speaking to the believers, the children of God, and the church. Paul says in 1 Corinthians chapter 12, that we all have a part to play in representing Christ. Some of us might be the right hand and others of us might be the left hand. So when Jesus tells them to not let the *"left hand know what your right hand is doing,"* He is talking about us, as the church, not boosting to other members of the body of Christ the good things we have done for the needy.

Physically, we cannot do a thing with our right hand that our left hand cannot do because our mind is connected. This helps us know and understand that Jesus, the Head of the church, knows what we are doing and will connect and work in unity with the amazing things He has planned.

Have you ever witnessed when you did a good deed (gave to someone that was in need) that you later saw how the dots connected? Maybe, that person got saved. Maybe, it was the one act that helped them believe God was listening to their prayer. Maybe, you have not seen the results and in your head you might even be wondering, "Did it do any good, and did God use it?" The confidence we have in knowing that Jesus, who is God, does see what each of us is doing is special. When we give according to how the Holy Spirit leads we can be sure to know that it will be revealed one day how God saw fit to use it.

Take some time today and ask God if there is anything He wants you to give to someone in need. It does not have to always be about money. Maybe God has blessed you financially and maybe He has blessed you with time. Ask God how He wants to use the gifts and blessings He has given you to bless someone else. It might be a kind word of encouragement. It could be a hand of friendship. It may be a warm hug for a dear brother or sister. The key is whatever that act of kindness or gift to the needy might be, we do it to help people see the awesome and amazing God that we serve. Listen to the Holy Spirit and respond to what He tells you to do.

EARTHLY REWARDS
DEVOTION #4 - PASTOR JOHN CARTER

"Thus, when you give to the needy, sound no trumpet before you, as the hypocrites do in the synagogues and in the streets, that they may be praised by others. Truly, I say to you, they have received their reward." Matthew 6:2

This is going to be a back-and-forth week. We first talked about what it means "to be seen" versus "unseen." Now we are going to walk through the differences between earthly rewards versus heavenly rewards. Today's focus is strictly on the earthly rewards that Jesus points us to in Matthew chapter 6. The conversation here begins with giving to the needy. I know the immediate thought is we are talking about financially giving to someone who is in need. I want you to consider other needs that may exist in someone's life that are of significantly more value than money.

I can come up with a few: (See Romans 12:6-9 if you want to look up some other ways you might be able to give.)

- Need for companionship or friendship
- Need for encouragement
- Need for council or life direction
- Need for forgiveness

I think there are many ways in which the Spirit leads us to give and it is not always about money.

As we read the verse for today, we see Jesus giving examples of hypocrites who give in an outward and visible manner. Can you think of any current examples that might relate to this example in the Scriptures? How about when people announce how much charity they give to a certain disaster or cause? Maybe you have heard someone boasting about how they gave some good advice to someone and it helped them? If you really pay attention, you can actually see this kind of boasting all around.

As we stated earlier, the contrast between receiving a heavenly reward to that of an earthly reward is dramatic. Consider the differences between things that are heavenly and things that are earthly. Let us walk through the earthly things and evaluate them. James, Jesus' brother, does a great job of walking us through the earthly motivations that might correlate to earthly gain.

In James 3:14-16, he wrote, *"But if you have bitter jealousy and selfish ambition in your hearts, do not boast and be false to the truth. This is not the wisdom that comes down from above, but is earthly, unspiritual, demonic. For where jealousy and selfish ambition exist, there will be disorder and every vile practice."*

Verse 14 kind of hammers it home. Now, when you re-read Matthew 6:2, you can see the motive of the hypocrites, worse yet they do it covered or shrouded in the cloak of godliness and righteousness. It is never fun talking about the difficult things in Scripture, often times as we reflect on ourselves and our own motives, we really need to be careful that we are not looking and operating with the earthly motives of selfish ambition. Take some time today and examine your motives and your heart. Ask God to show you where you have been operating and doing things to receive earthly rewards. Let me leave you with some more from James. May this encourage you as you walk through this passage of Scripture.

James 4:7-8 says, *"Submit yourselves therefore to God. Resist the devil, and he will flee from you. Draw near to God, and he will draw near to you."*

HEAVENLY REWARDS
DEVOTION #5 - PASTOR JOHN CARTER

"But when you give to the needy, do not let your left hand know what your right hand is doing, so that your giving may be in secret. And your Father who sees in secret will reward you."
Matthew 6:3-4

Have you ever done something in secret? If we are 100% honest, we would admit that most of the things we do in secret we do because we are too ashamed for them to be revealed to the world. I love how Jesus flips everything upside down in this aspect of giving to the needy. While normally doing something amazing and kind, like giving to the needy, is something that we would not even care if it was known, Jesus tells us to keep it secret. In fact, the things we are inclined to keep secret because we are ashamed, Jesus tells us to confess them! This whole scenario seems backward. Keep secret the good things, but confess the things we want to hide.

He continues to articulate the reward of doing such things as being heavenly rewards from the Father. This week we have been walking through Matthew 6:1-4. Take a moment and read the passage.

Matthew 6:1-4 says, *"Beware of practicing your righteousness before other people in order to be seen by them, for then you will have no reward from your Father who is in heaven. Thus, when you give to the needy, sound no trumpet before you, as the hypocrites do in the synagogues and in the streets, that they may be praised by others. Truly, I say to you, they have received their reward. But when you give to the needy, do not let your left hand know what your right hand is doing, so that your giving may be in secret. And your Father who sees in secret will reward you."*

It starts with this idea of practicing our righteousness before other people, and it ends with rewards that the Father will give us. I want to go back to James and look at what he is teaching us about the contrasting ideas of Heaven and Earth.

James 3:17-18 adds, *"But the wisdom from above is first pure, then peaceable, gentle, open to reason, full of mercy and good fruits, impartial and sincere. And a harvest of righteousness is sown in peace by those who make peace."*

Pay particular attention to verse 18 and the *"harvest of righteousness."* The harvest can also be the reward. When we are striving for heavenly rewards, we see the importance of how God works. I love that James includes the concept of sowing in peace. In Matthew, Jesus is talking about how we give in secret and the reward comes from the *"Father who sees in secret."*

Ask yourself this, "How am I sowing peace today?" It is hard to sow anything in peace if you do not have any peace to begin with. When our hearts' motives are examined and we are walking in the way of our Heavenly Father, there is a peace that *"surpasses all understanding"* we as believers get to experience.

Philippians 4:7 says, *"And the peace of God, which surpasses all understanding, will guard your hearts and your minds in Christ Jesus."*

While Jesus is walking us through our motive of giving to the needy, take this moment and ask yourself if you have made peace with God, who sees in secret. I started by asking you if you have ever done anything in secret. Most of the time we do those things in secret because we are ashamed. Have you considered that nothing is secret to God and Jesus? The ultimate reward we can receive is the gift of being with God forever and having the acceptance and recognition of our Heavenly Father.

If you are a believer and you are reading this devotion, consider the awesome blessing and reward of the Father we have received in His Son, Jesus. He is the One who knows all the secret things and yet chooses to take the cross on our behalf. If you are reading this and struggling to find peace, not really sure if there is a reward for walking in the way of the Lord, can I encourage you to just talk to God (He knows it all)? He knows all the secrets of life, both good and bad. Take some time to talk to Him and confess the things you are ashamed of. Receive the reward of peace that comes from being in a relationship with God.

HYPOCRISY VS. AUTHENTICITY IN CHARITY

DEVOTION #5 - PASTOR JOHN CARTER

Matthew 6:1-4 summarizes for us the difference between hypocrisy and authenticity, particularly in the area of our giving. Maybe as we walk through these verses you have found yourself on one side or the other of this coin. Are you living as a hypocrite or walking in an authentic relationship with Christ? Those are the two choices. Jesus never seems to mince words or leave a person guessing about what He means.

Matthew 6:1-4 says, *"Beware of practicing your righteousness before other people in order to be seen by them, for then you will have no reward from your Father who is in heaven. Thus, when you give to the needy, sound no trumpet before you, as the hypocrites do in the synagogues and in the streets, that they may be praised by others. Truly, I say to you, they have received their reward. But when you give to the needy, do not let your left hand know what your right hand is doing, so that your giving may be in secret. And your Father who sees in secret will reward you."*

You do not really need me to expound on this text any more than we already have in the previous devotions. It really comes down to your own decision of whether you are going to be authentic or going to be a hypocrite. We have examined the motives of being seen by others versus being seen by God. We have walked through the earthly rewards that come from being seen by others versus the rewards that come from working through the secret things in our hearts. If all we do is read and gain some kind of factual or intellectual knowledge without ever changing the way we operate, then we do not really live in truth and authenticity.

If you look at the etymology of the word "charity" it ultimately comes down to love. In Scripture, we read there are two great commandments that we as believers are to operate under. Mark 12:30-31 says, **"'And you shall love the Lord your God with all your heart and with all your soul and with all your mind and with all your strength.' The second is this: 'You shall love your neighbor as yourself.' There is no other commandment greater than these."**

In Matthew 6:1-4, Jesus is teaching us how to authentically love God and love our neighbors (brothers). He desires that we, like children, will listen to His instructions and learn to walk in the manner that He has taught us to operate. Just like kids, we can choose. We can choose to obey and listen or choose our own way. My hope and prayer this week is that as you have examined the Scriptures, you have taken time to choose to be authentic and genuine in your heart. This includes admitting our shortcomings and being encouraged in the person of Jesus.

As we looked at the differences between showing and living out the genuine love of God, it is ultimately a personal decision. It is something that stems from the depth of the heart. It is a decision that comes from a personal understanding of what we have received as followers of Jesus. Jesus left an example for us in this love that we are so desperately trying to mimic and live out in our own lives.

John 15:13-14 says, **"Greater love has no one than this, that someone lay down his life for his friends. You are my friends if you do what I command you."**

Ultimately, God will be the one who knows the difference in the way you show your love. He will know whether it was authentic or for some ulterior motive. His desire is that His children operate and behave in a manner that is genuine and authentic. His desire is that the "charity" (love) we show is an example of the very love He showed us; in that, we give and obey what Jesus showed us in His Word.

LESSON TWO

The Tone
of Prayer

PASTOR CHUCK LINDSEY

"And when you pray, you shall not be like the hypocrites. For they love to pray standing in the synagogues and on the corners of the streets, that they may be seen by men. Assuredly, I say to you, they have their reward. But you, when you pray, go into your room, and when you have shut your door, pray to your Father who is in the secret place; and your Father who sees in secret will reward you openly." Matthew 6:5-6 (NKJV)

"And when you pray, you shall not be like the hypocrites. For they love to pray standing in the synagogues and on the corners of the streets, that they may be seen by men. Assuredly, I say to you, they have their reward." Matthew 6:5 (NKJV)

We move from false giving to false prayer. Jesus warns against praying the way that the *"hypocrites"* *"pray."* *"Hypocrites"* comes from the Greek word "hupokrites" which means mask wearers. *"Pray"* comes from the Greek word "proseúchomai" which means "to ask."

1. How could one be hypocritical in prayer?

   _____

   _____

   _____

2. Are you comfortable praying out loud in a group? Why or why not?

   _____

   _____

   _____

The word *"pray"* conveys the idea that you are going to the Lord for some need (encouragement, help, counsel, or strength). So the Lord says to us when you come to Me for something, do not (ever) *"be."* *"Be"* comes from the Greek word "ésomai" which means to be (like) this.

Jesus tells us to not be at all like them. What are they like? He tells us. They are the "mask-wearers." **"Love"** comes from the Greek word "phileo" which means "to be deeply fond of." They find a lot of pleasure in a very specific way of praying. They **"love"** to **"pray standing."** **"Standing"** comes from the Greek word "hístēmi" which means "be standing so that you can be seen."

Jesus says that what they **"love"** is to be **"seen."** To accomplish this, they **"stand"** in the *"synagogues and on the corners of the streets"* to be seen by as many people as possible. Interestingly, the word **"stand"** there in Greek is written in the perfect tense which means that *this* is where they do their **"praying."** In other words, it is the only place they pray! It is clear in what Jesus says that what they **"love"** is not the Lord they are "praying" to, but rather, the way this makes them look to others.

3. Where are some places that you pray?

_____

_____

_____

Jesus says, their goal is to be **"seen."** **"Seen"** is the Greek word "phaínō" which means "to appear to be." Their desire was to appear to be something that they are not. They want people to think they are spiritual, godly, and close to God when they are not at all.

The next key word is **"says."** **"Says"** is the Greek verb "lego" (no, not the plastic bricks) which means "to collect thoughts, organize and then speak them."

Jesus says, *"They have their reward."* **"Have"** comes from the Greek verb "apecho" which means "payment made in full."

Jesus says that the reward of people seeing them is, in fact, their full *"reward."* None other shall be given from Him! What an incredibly tragic trade this is! It is like Esau of the Old Testament trading his entire birthright and position within the tribe of his family for a bowl of boiled lentils (Genesis 25).

When you pray, do not be like them, to be seen by people! For in so doing, we trade real reward for what does not satisfy.

"But you, when you pray, go into your room, and when you have shut your door, pray to your Father who is in the secret place; and your Father who sees in secret will reward you openly." Matthew 6:6 (NKJV)

The words *"but you"* should not be skipped over. Jesus is making a distinction between these false believers or mask-wearers, and you and me who are His people. They would not listen to His instruction. We do. They continued to promote themselves and point to themselves. We do not. This is because we are His people.

His instruction, on how to pray correctly begins with the words *"when you pray."* "**Pray**" comes from the Greek verb "proseúchomai" which means "to ask."

Notice that He did not say, "If you pray?" For us, as His people, it is not an "if" but rather a *"when." "When you pray"* sets us apart from the Pharisees as those who are actually coming to Him and actually praying to Him. We are not going through religious motions. It is real. We come to Him, Who is real, with real requests and real worship.

We come now to the details of how to actually pray. We are to do the opposite of the hypocrites. Rather than publicly drawing attention to ourselves in prayer. We are to find somewhere private (*"secretly"*) to **"go"** (the Greek verb "eisérchomai") and when you have **"shut"** (the Greek verb "kleíō") the door (emphasizing when no one else is watching), then *"pray to your Father."* Note that it is not wrong to pray in public. It is the attitude in which we pray that Jesus is addressing. Who are we praying to? What are we praying for? What are we really seeking? That is what Jesus is getting at here. He is not condemning all public prayer or prayer meetings. He is condemning the false praying of these religious charlatans.

4. How can praying out loud with others at a restaurant be a good thing?

_____
_____
_____

5. How can praying out loud with others at a restaurant be inappropriate?

_____
_____
_____

Please notice that the emphasis in Jesus' words is on God being our *"Father."* This is critical to understand in order to pray correctly. Lest we think we are being too informal or irreverent in addressing God as our Father, this picture is how God Himself has chosen to describe Himself to us. It is meant to convey His attentiveness to our praying and His willingness to hear us when we call out to Him for whatever we may need.

6. How is viewing God as *"Father"* comforting?

_____
_____
_____

This is further emphasized by the words Jesus used when He said that the *"Father"* "<u>sees</u>" (the Greek verb "blépō"). It is a word that means He *actually* sees us as we pray. The contrast could not be clearer. Jesus is saying that the hypocrites pray to be seen by people, but we as His people pray and are seen by Him! Do you think of God as your Father who watches you as you pray? As a father, I would often slightly open my eyes to watch my children as they prayed. When I saw their eyes tightly closed and hands clenched together, speaking in earnest to our Lord, it blessed me. He does the same. He sees you and knows your need completely and loves when you come to Him. It is so much so, that one day, He *"will reward."*

7. Do you have a "secret place" to pray?

_____

_____

_____

8. Where are some places that could be a good "secret place"?

_____

_____

_____

"Reward" comes from the Greek verb "apodídōmi" which means "to give from one's own desires."

The promise is that He will *"reward you openly."* Just close your eyes for a moment and try to imagine what it will be like for your Father to (one day) reward you in front of countless angels and others, expressing His love and acceptance of you! What a day that will be! In 1 Corinthians 2:9 (NKJV), we read, *"Eye has not seen, nor ear heard, nor have entered into the heart of man the things which God has prepared for those who love Him."*

9. What do you think the *"reward"* ceremony will be like?

_____

_____

_____

When you pray to your Father, even in secret, He watches and knows. He will bless you openly one day!

NOTES

PRAYER
DEVOTION #1 - PASTOR JOHN CARTER

As we walk through Matthew chapter 6 this week, we are going to look at the specifics of prayer. Prayer is an amazing topic to study in the Bible. Prayer is talked about all through Scripture. From the Old Testament to the New Testament, we see the importance of prayer being a constant. This week, we are going to observe the distinction between a prideful person and the person who intently seeks God in their prayer. It looks different, feels different, and has dramatically different results.

In preparation for this week, I found this passage in Chronicles to be a powerful Scripture to consider before we dive into Matthew 6:5-6. In 2 Chronicles 7:14, we read, *"If my people who are called by my name humble themselves, and pray and seek my face and turn from their wicked ways, then I will hear from heaven and will forgive their sin and heal their land."*

I think this passage in Chronicles is a great Old Testament passage that Jesus will walk us through this week in Matthew chapter 6. The main idea is really understanding the tone of our prayer to God.

You are going to see the elements of pride versus humility in prayer. It is the difference between prayer for selfish motives versus the power of prayer that comes from seeking God's face. You are going to be challenged to turn from things that are not right. God has a way of pointing out those wrong and wicked things we so desperately want to hang on to. Ultimately, you are going to learn that prayer is so much more than just saying, "Hey!" to God. There is the power of forgiveness that comes from rightly approaching God, and there is healing that comes from walking in step with the instructions He gives us for prayer. This week, you are going to walk through Jesus' very words on how we ought to pray.

In preparation, start by setting aside time every day to talk to God. I would encourage you to do this before anything else in the day gets started. It might mean you set the alarm clock 30 minutes earlier than normal. Every person is different and the schedules of all do not necessarily match up, but make sure the first thing you do is take time to be with God. As we read in Chronicles, we need to seek His face. Make it a priority despite all the responsibilities you may have this week. If you are a new believer and you are not really sure how prayer even works, just sit quietly, be still for a moment, and ask God to prepare your heart for how you can be better connected and in communion with Him. Ask God to show you how you can improve and better understand how to approach Him, learn, and hear from Him.

I will conclude today with some words from Hebrews. The passage is meant to be words of encouragement. As believers in Christ, we should encourage each other to walk in a way that is honoring and pleasing to God. It is designed so that we would not fall for the lies of sins, but hold true to the person of Jesus Christ. When we hear His voice calling to us, we would not reject it, but we would humble ourselves to His voice and listing to what He wants to teach and share with us.

Hebrews 3:12-15 says, ***"Take care, brothers, lest there be in any of you an evil, unbelieving heart, leading you to fall away from the living God. But exhort one another every day, as long as it is called 'today,' that none of you may be hardened by the deceitfulness of sin. For we have come to share in Christ, if indeed we hold our original confidence firm to the end. As it is said, 'Today, if you hear his voice, do not harden your hearts as in the rebellion.'"***

TO BE SEEN IN PRAYER
DEVOTION #2 - PASTOR JOHN CARTER

Some of you will be able to relate to the story I am about to share. If you grew up in church, at some point you gathered around food and someone was asked to bless the food for all those present. Now as a kid, my hunger always seemed to control me. When someone would pray for the food, I always had the thought, "Man, hurry up; I am so hungry!"

I also noticed that there were some who, when they prayed, seemed to pray about things other than the food. This really annoyed me as a hungry little boy. It was like a whole sermon in a prayer (a mini sermon if you will). I am not here to criticize the way people pray or what they pray about. I am simply talking about how sometimes when we say we are praying to God, we are actually praying in a way that other people hear us.

Matthew 6:5 says, *"And when you pray, you must not be like the hypocrites. For they love to stand and pray in the synagogues and at the street corners, that they may be seen by others."*

This week we are going to walk through the contrast between genuine prayer and disingenuous prayer. As we dwell on the verse written above, we can clearly see the instruction of Jesus is to contrast one's actions with the motives of their heart. Examining the manner in which we pray is less important than examining the motive by which we pray. In other words, are you talking to God or are you talking for someone that is in the crowd or maybe in earshot of your prayer? It is interesting that Jesus points out the visual in something that is mostly an act of audio. He says that hypocrites love to be seen by others.

Have you ever considered how people view you in your prayers? Let me go one step further. What about when you tell someone you will "pray for them"? Is that genuine or is that something you just say to make the other person feel good? Ouch! That hurt!

I want to share a story that I think perfectly encapsulates the point of today's devotion.

We were going to one of the many activities we have at The River Church. This particular activity involved kids and I invited a family to come and hang out at this kids' activity. I had spent some time with the Dad of the child and there were several times when I expressed that I would be praying for him and his family. We were all in the car and the little child said she has a question she wanted to ask me. I am always eager to hear the inquisitive mind of a child. I do not think there is anything in the Word to help prepare me for what she proceeded to ask me! "Pastor John, when you say you are going to pray for us, do you really mean it? Or are you just saying it to make us feel better?"

A nine-year-old child had already been exposed to the hypocrisy of the church. Man, my heart broke for that little girl. She was intuitive as she had already seen the difference between one who just says something versus someone who actually does what they say they will do!

You can be sure that I prayed with a whole new fervency after that conversation.

Today's devotion is all about examining the motive of our prayers. Is it to be seen by others? Is it to make others feel better about themselves, or is there a genuine heart to go to the Almighty God and put our petitions before Him? Do we approach God with the faith that He cares to hear and listen to us? Do we make time dedicated to talking to our Heavenly Father? Take some time today, one-on-one with God! If you told people you would pray for them, then do it! The time we get to be with God is worth more than anything else we could ever have.

POWER OF SECRET PRAYER
DEVOTION #3 - PASTOR JOHN CARTER

Have you ever been in conversation with someone that seemed distracted? Was their attention on the device that was in front of them? Were they busy playing video games and it seemed like the only way you can get their attention was to stand right in front of the TV? Are you naturally intuitive enough to see their mind is somewhere else and you notice you do not have their full attention? How does that make you feel?

As we walk through the genuine heart of prayer, Jesus does a fantastic job of giving us a comparison. It is a bad example, if you will, versus a good example. Yesterday, we looked at the bad example (the way the hypocrites pray). Today, we are going to walk through the example that Jesus articulates for us to help us focus our conversations directly on God. I do not think God is completely indifferent to how we approach Him. In fact, being that we are made in His image, just as we desire the attention of someone we are engaged in conversation with, I believe God also desires this devoted attention.

Matthew 6:6 says, ***"But when you pray, go into your room and shut the door and pray to your Father who is in secret."***

We should consider prayer as a time of communication with God. Yes, it is with God! He is the One who made and created all things, the One who has the power to speak things into existence. He is the supreme being of all beings ever created! Considering that, it is amazing that God offers us time to come to Him and talk with Him. I think it would be okay to say He might desire focused attention. Jesus gives us this picture of going into a room and praying behind closed doors, the comparison is the contrast of being seen and heard by people versus being seen and heard by the Almighty. God knows all things, but He still desires to have a relationship with us.

I love that Jesus treats prayer as a special time. It is a time that requires you to close the door. Have you ever been praying and as you were talking to God, weird things pop up into your head? Maybe it had to do with things that are going to happen in the day or maybe it was a thought of what you were going to eat. Maybe you have a really bad attention span and you see something on the wall and your mind drifts. In the passage above, Jesus says to shut the door and pray! I see this as Jesus instructing us to close out all the distractions of the world. When we come to the Father, He wants our attention. He wants our focus to be on the petitions we bring to Him. He wants our focus to be on Him.

Have you ever considered your prayer time with God as a date? I know this may seem like a weird analogy, but try and walk through the thought exercise for a minute. I try to take my three daughters on a date once a month. They are so excited to get to spend time with me. It is special for me too. They cherish every moment and all the conversations we have are very focused. As I see their heart and their passions, I get the feeling this is also the desire of our Heavenly Father. He desires to know our hearts and our passions, an intimate moment where we can be in the presence of our Father and He gives us His undivided attention.

He asks us to do this in secret because our Father is in secret. The humility of God is expressed in the very way we pray. God is not bragging to His other kids about how much time He spends with one versus the other. He is saying, "I devote myself to my children and I care for each of them."

The power of Elisha's prayer for healing brought back a child to life. In 2 Kings 4:32-33, we read, *"When Elisha came into the house, he saw the child lying dead on his bed. So he went in and shut the door behind the two of them and prayed to the Lord."*

Isaiah tells us the power of prayer in repentance protects us from the fury of God.

Isaiah 26:20 says, *"Come, my people, enter your chambers, and shut your doors behind you; hide yourselves for a little while until the fury has passed by."*

Taking the time to literally shut the door and go to a place where it is just you and God can produce incredible results in our relationship with God. It allows God to work on things in our hearts that need to be fixed or felt. It allows our prayers to reach the One and Only being that can produce miraculous results in our petitions. Let me encourage you today to try this practice in real life. Find a place where the world can be shut out (do not take your phone there) and just focus on you and God. Let Him speak to you as you pour your heart out to Him.

REWARD OF BEING SEEN BY GOD
DEVOTION #4 - PASTOR JOHN CARTER

"But when you pray, go into your room and shut the door and pray to your Father who is in secret. And your Father who sees in secret will reward you." Matthew 6:6

Yesterday, we read about the awesome privilege we have of walking through intimate time with God. In our time and age, distractions are ever so present. It can include your phone going off all the time, news feeds blowing up, trying to see everything, and being connected to all that is happening with friends and family. That time with God can easily be put off to an "I will get to it later" conversation.

The later part of this verse is a common theme throughout these few verses. Last week, we talked about the rewards of giving in secret. Here we see Jesus teaching us the rewards of praying in secret. Consider what is being talked about here for a moment. God says come to me in a private conversation and share your heart with me. Let me work on your heart so that we can be better connected. I can share with you some areas that you need to work on and you can cast your burdens on Me. The promise is that God will reward us for diligently coming to Him.

James 5:15-16 records, *"And the prayer of faith will save the one who is sick, and the Lord will raise him up. And if he has committed sins, he will be forgiven. Therefore, confess your sins to one another and pray for one another, that you may be healed. The prayer of a righteous person has great power as it is working."* Considering the writings and teaching of James. I believe there are two parts to this.

1. The correction and power to overcome sin.
2. The power of God to answer our petitions.

This reward that Jesus promises us is profound. First, the forgiveness of sins and the power to overcome those sins only can come from God. When you are in that secret place with God, deal with the sins that God points out to you. Do not just ignore them! God is pointing them out to you for a reason, for your good. How long will you ignore the reproof and correction of God? He promises to forgive you, but you must turn away from the sin. Look at what James is saying; go to the Lord in prayer not just for yourself, but for your brothers and sisters in Christ. Pray for the brother who is battling sin or struggling through the grip and hold of the devil. The One who can give us the power to overcome it is God and Jesus Himself.

Sickness is a common reason for people to come to the Lord in prayer. If you have been a part of a prayer chain or a Wednesday night prayer meeting, most of the time it is filled with requests to heal or petitions of those who are hurting. This might even be why you are interested in this series because you are looking for the right way to fix a problem. It may be an illness or sickness that is profoundly affecting you. The power that can heal only comes from God, the One who can make it better. The One to fix it is God. I know God is the one that can forgive. He is the one who can heal, and He has all the power in the world. The question that always comes to mind for me is, "Why is He always the last person I go to?"

Maybe there is something specific you need prayer for today. You might be dealing with sin, sickness, or just a struggle in general. Let me encourage you, there is a place that you can go to get peace and hope for the situation. If you want additional brothers and sisters to pray for you, let me encourage you to reach out by texting "riverconnect" to 97000 and follow the instructions for a prayer request. As we see in James, we are instructed to carry the burdens together with the confidence that the One who can fix them hears them and He will reward us.

I love that James says, *"The prayer of a righteous person has great power as it is working."* That phase *"as it is working"* implies that prayer sometimes takes time and does not just happen in the immediate moment. Trust in Jesus and the Father to know that He hears and He knows what is best for each and every one of us.

REWARD OF BEING SEEN BY MEN
DEVOTION #5 - PASTOR JOHN CARTER

"And when you pray, you must not be like the hypocrites. For they love to stand and pray in the synagogues and at the street corners, that they may be seen by others. Truly, I say to you, they have received their reward." Matthew 6:5

At the beginning of the week, we looked at the contrast between being seen by men versus being seen by God. Yesterday, we very briefly walked through the reward that comes from God. Ultimately, He is the One who has the power to heal and the power to forgive. He should be our first and primary place to go when it comes to confession of sins and petitions for healing.

What about the other way of praying? There is praying for the sake of others hearing us. There is danger in the prideful desire to have others hear us pray or even praying for someone else just to give off the impression that we are "super righteous" and close to God. Maybe you have even heard this said, "Can you pray for me because it seems like God answers your prayer?"

Compare the response Jesus gives to the prideful, arrogant person that is only self-seeking in his prayer. Jesus says they got their reward. In other words, they did not connect with the One who can actually heal, they did not connect with the One who can actually forgive. Their reward was that people saw them and they may have a small sense of glory for a moment. However, they have no power, they have no authority to forgive or release the bondage of sins. Their rewards are self-serving.

Do not be like them! This is what Jesus is saying. I know it seems obvious and you are probably thinking to yourself, "Never! I will never do this!" I hope this is true, but I want to look at some practical challenges for this.

When was the last time you spent time with God alone and prayed for your spouse? I mean, really prayed for their struggles and sins and sickness. When was the last time you spent time alone in a quiet, undistracted place with God praying for your children or grandchildren? Yes, it stings me, too. However, this is what is talked about in James 5:16, *"Therefore, confess your sins to one another and pray for one another, that you may be healed. The prayer of a righteous person has great power as it is working."*

The *"one another"* there is meant to help us not be so self-centered in our prayers to God. Maybe today you need to devote some time, to not make your prayer all about you, but for a fellow brother or sister in Christ that really needs the amazing power of God to do a miracle for them. Go to your quiet place and lift them up, carry their needs and burdens; take them to the very place that has hope! Take them to the One who has all the authority to forgive, and all the power to heal.

HYPOCRITICAL VS. AUTHENTIC PRAYER
DEVOTION #6 - PASTOR JOHN CARTER

As we continue to dive into this chapter of Matthew, we will keep looking at the comparison and contrast of hypocrisy versus real (authentic) believers who are walking according to the Word of God. This week we see Jesus comparing and contrasting the ways in which we pray.

Maybe this week the Holy Spirit convicted you of a sin or a lack of time with God. The first step in fixing something is to identify the problem. Once a problem has been identified, we need to commit it to the Lord and continually seek Him. Jesus was teaching His disciples in the garden this very thing. In the midst of trials and difficulties, we need to make sure we are going to the only One that has all the power to forgive and the power to heal.

Matthew 26:41 says, *"Watch and pray that you may not enter into temptation. The spirit indeed is willing, but the flesh is weak."*

The warning Jesus is telling us that our flesh is a force to be reconned with. We need to continually be taking time to be alone with God and making sure we are not distracted by outside influences. In the disciples' case, the outside influence was sleep. Taking time to be alone with God can be a place of rest and comfort, but we need to be diligent to put "one another's" burdens before God.

Paul also teaches us Who we can go to when it comes to the power of prayer.

Ephesians 1:15-21 says, *"For this reason, because I have heard of your faith in the Lord Jesus and your love toward all the saints, I do not cease to give thanks for you, remembering you in my prayers, that the God of our Lord Jesus Christ, the Father of glory, may give you the Spirit of wisdom and of revelation in the knowledge of him, having the eyes of your hearts enlightened, that you may know what is the hope to which he has called you, what are the riches of his glorious inheritance in the saints, and what is the immeasurable greatness of his power toward us who believe, according to the working of his great might that he worked in Christ when he raised him from the dead and seated him at his right hand in the heavenly places, far above all rule and authority and power and dominion, and above every name that is named, not only in this age but also in the one to come."*

These are passages of serious encouragement! Our faith in Jesus Christ and the love we have for each other should be a source of hope, knowledge, and wisdom for the awesome privilege we have in serving God the Father. Jesus is the One who sits at the right hand of God. He has been given authority, power, and dominion in our lives. to do great things in our lives to change our wicked hearts to be drawn closer to Him. This promise that Paul so eloquently points out is not just for the age Paul lived in but also for the age we live in. It is for right now!

Be encouraged this week that God is not silent! He is not deaf! He reigns and rules. Hopefully, He has shown you something to work on. I pray and hope as we continue to study through Matthew chapter 6, He will continue to encourage and draw you closer to Him. Desire that He will open your hearts to His powerful truth and the amazing love He has for you.

LESSON THREE

The Wording
of Prayer

PASTOR CHUCK LINDSEY

"And when you pray, do not use vain repetitions as the heathen do. For they think that they will be heard for their many words. Therefore do not be like them. For your Father knows the things you have need of before you ask Him." Matthew 6:7-8 (NKJV)

Jesus continues in His instruction on how to pray and says, ***"And when you pray*** (from the Greek verb "proseúchomai") ***do not use vain repetitions as the heathen do."***

"Vain repetitions" comes from the Greek word "battologéō" and means "to babble, chatter." This is a word that describes useless speaking. It is empty words that are spoken over and over, yet really mean nothing.

1. What could be some ***"vain repetitions"*** we use today?

Grace, public prayer →

_____

_____

We do not have to guess as to why they were doing this. Jesus tells us, ***"For they think that they will be heard for their many words."*** ***"Think"*** comes from the Greek word "dokéō" and means "to think, imagine." ***"Heard"*** comes from the Greek word "eisakoúō" and means "to give attention to, listen to."

The warning here is actually against something that was often seen in pagan ("heathen" comes from the Greek word "ethnikós" and means nations) worship practices. Words were chanted over and over ad infinitum to garner the notice of whatever deity was being prayed to. The same practice is still seen today in many Eastern religions. Jesus tells us, as His people, that this is not at all necessary. He hears us when we pray.

2. In its purest form, what is prayer?

_____

_____

_____

"Therefore __do not be like__ them." Jesus says that we do not need to pray over and over the same words hoping to be heard. He hears us. Some people have the idea that God is busy. They think that He has a lot going on and could not possibly tune into their "little" request. Some even have the idea that they would not bug the "Man upstairs" until it is a big need; then I will put in my request! Many have the idea that to get God's attention; they have to continually repeat the request. It is the idea that there are millions of people offering requests all at the same time and the only way to get mine "through" is to say it constantly. Hear Jesus' words today, *"__Do not be like__ them"* these "<u>repetitions</u>" are not needed to get His attention. He hears your request with full attention and as though you were the only one asking anything of Him. We are His children and He is our Father. Jesus assures us that we have His undivided attention.

3. How is it comforting to know He hears us the first time?

_____

_____

_____

4. Is it good to pray for the same thing more than once? Why or why not?

_____

_____

_____

Jesus drives this point home with the remainder of verse 8 which says, *"For"* (this is why you do not need to repeat over and over and beg) *"your Father __knows__* (from the Greek verb "eídō" and means "to see completely") *the things you have need of before you __ask__* (from the Greek verb "aitéō" and means to "ask, request, seeking by the inferior from the superior") *Him."*

5. If God knows before we ask, why do we need to pray?

_____

_____

_____

Wow! What a promise! Not only do we not have to beg God repetitiously to get Him to notice our need, but here we are told that He knows what we need before we know what we need. So this brings about a question I have been asked many times that goes like this, "If God already knows what we need before we ask, why do we need to ask?" My answer to that question is usually, "First, we do not *need* to, we *get* to. Secondly, He wants us to talk to Him."

An illustration here is helpful. I love my children. I often know what they need before they ask me. However, I want them to ask me because of the connection it creates between my children and me. When they ask, they are admitting their need; they are looking to me, their father, as the one that can supply that need. I, as their father, see their need and engage in love to either correct, counsel, or meet that need. It is the basis of a relationship. Prayer is not about getting, it is about a relationship. As we go to our Father, we necessarily humble ourselves and admit our needs. He, seeing our needs, lovingly engages to speak, correct, counsel, or meet our needs. Amazingly, James 4:2 (NKJV) seems to indicate that our Father limits His action to our asking. It says, ***"You do not have because you do not ask."*** Our Father wisely withholds from us certain things, to teach us, to grow us, and to remove our pride and independence that says, "I can do this without you." He often restrains what He would want to do for us until we humble ourselves, see our need, and then ask Him. As a dad, I have done the same with my children. I will often give my kids tasks that are just beyond their ability for this reason. "Judah (who is currently 10 years old), drag that large box full of wood scraps to the front for the trash man to take it." Judah's eager reply, "Okay!" Now, I know how heavy it is because I packed it. It is well over 100 pounds. Admittedly, there are two things I want to have to happen with a request like this. First, I want Judah to try! I want him to feel how heavy it is and try to do something that is difficult. I want him to pull it, push it, or figure out some way of moving that box. I want him to solve problems. Secondly, if he cannot figure out a way, I want him to call my name. I want him to ask me for help. I want him to say, "Dad, I cannot figure it out. Help me!" When he does that, I will stride over to him, pretend to be the strongest person who has ever lived, and help him drag it. We will drag it together. It is the relationship that I am after. That is the goal. So Jesus tells us, "Just ask because I hear you."

6. How is this illustration helpful?

_____

_____

_____

7. Have you ever written out your prayers? How could this be helpful?

_____

_____

_____

Jesus says, "You do not have to say it over and over, I hear you. In fact, I know what you need before you do, so just ask."

NOTES

HE HEARS AND HAS POWER
DEVOTION #1 - PASTOR JOHN CARTER

We are going to continue our study of Matthew chapter 6 and look intently at Jesus' teaching regarding how our words matter to God. What we say and what we do makes a difference in how we approach the Almighty. We are going to walk through Matthew 6:7-8 this week focusing on the words of prayer. As we explore what Jesus is teaching us, I want to draw your attention to a passage in 1 Kings. Many of you may know this story in Scripture where a major victory was won for the prophet of God. This is one of my favorite accounts of history. Elijah basically calls out the people of God and says, "Hey, we need to stop pretending." In other words, we need to be authentic. If God is real, then let us worship and obey Him. If Baal is real, then worship and obey him. I have this idea to put them to the test. If you have time this week read 1 Kings chapter 18. You will find it profoundly comforting to know that we have a God that can hear us and has the power to respond to us.

Without giving the whole story away, I want to share just a snippet of the story. Over 800 prophets of Baal are trying to accomplish the task set before them to try and show that Baal is real. In 1 Kings 18:26, we read, *"And they took the bull that was given them, and they prepared it and called upon the name of Baal from morning until noon, saying, 'O Baal, answer us!' But there was no voice, and no one answered. And they limped around the altar that they had made."* In 1 Kings 18:29, he continues, *"And as midday passed, they raved on until the time of the offering of the oblation, but there was no voice. No one answered; no one paid attention."*

This was the result of their pleading to a god with no voice, power, or authority. As you read the passage in 1 Kings, you actually really feel for the prophets because they so desperately desired to believe in this "god" named Baal. They thought they had to approach him in a certain way. They had to do certain actions in order to get his attention. They were even willing to cut and pierce themselves to bleed out, just to get their god to respond. Yet, at the end of the day, they were left with no voice, answer, or god to respond to their pleas.

In the verses we are going to walk through this week, we are going to see Jesus addressing this ritualistic repeating of phrases as though they are magic spells. Jesus will talk about saying prayers as though you are addressing Congress using lofty words and repeating words as though it somehow makes God hear better. In a lot of ways, Jesus will contrast the difference between Baal and the God of Elijah.

If you have not guessed already, the God of Elijah showed up in a big way! He "burned the house down." Here is Elijah's prayer on Mt. Carmel from 1 Kings 18:37-39, ***"'Answer me, O Lord, answer me, that this people may know that you, O Lord, are God, and that you have turned their hearts back.' Then the fire of the Lord fell and consumed the burnt offering and the wood and the stones and the dust, and licked up the water that was in the trench. And when all the people saw it, they fell on their faces and said, 'The Lord, he is God; the Lord, he is God.'"***

I hope this is encouraging to you to know that when we are praying to God, Elijah's God, we are praying to the only God that hears and answers!

PRAYING AS THE GENTILES DO
DEVOTION #2 - PASTOR JOHN CARTER

Jesus continues to teach us to walk through the aspects of prayer.

Matthew 6:7 starts, ***"And when you pray, do not heap up empty phrases as the Gentiles do."***

What comes to your mind when you hear Jesus telling us not to pray like the Gentiles, heaping up empty phrases? First of all, this has very little to do with ethnicity, but more with methodology. Jesus was telling people not to pray in a certain method.

I spent 17 years of my life in a foreign country, Japan. One of the amazing, yet sad, aspects of the Japanese culture is the absolutely beautiful, but spiritually empty places called temples and shrines that exist all over the land. From the furthest northern region of Japan to the southernmost tip of the Island and all throughout the entire country, you will find temples dedicated to many different types of gods. Most of them have an image graven out of wood or stone to represent that particular god.

When I read this passage, I could not help but remember the sounds of Buddhist and Shinto priests praying to their gods in the temples. The prayer is more of a chant and it has a sense of rhythm to it. I have a very clear picture in my head of what this aspect of ***"empty phrases"*** means to me. If you have never traveled outside the United States, you may not have much to compare this idea to. Maybe you have spent your whole life in the church and all you have to compare is what you have heard either from the stage or when someone was praying a blessing over the food. If I can say this as kindly as I possibly can, let me tell you there were many empty phases all the time. I think of a culture far away from the United States and consider the literal graven images that people prayed to and have the sounds of repeated prayers of monks in my mind.

I have also heard the same form of prayer in the church. We often learn this aspect of prayer in the traditions of Sunday School. We tell our kids to fold their hands, close their eyes, and bow their heads. We often will teach them to start out with the phrase, "Dear Jesus," and the prayer is not done until someone says, "Amen."

We have our own heaps of empty phrases that we use to make our prayers sound super spiritual. As we looked at this aspect in previous weeks, oftentimes we find that we add these extra phases to make others who might hear, think we are really close to God.

Please do not misunderstand what I am saying. It is not wrong to teach our children reverence in prayer, I am not in any way trying to mock or ridicule any aspect of teaching our children the power of prayer and how to do it. All I am saying is that sometimes we can, with all good intentions, miss the boat. The prayers of the Japanese monks are rituals. They say them and memorize them all in hopes that their perfect execution of the prayer is what makes it heard. It is like the prophets of Baal we talked about yesterday. Having grown up in church, and being saved as an adult later in life, it was really hard for me not to revert back to praying the way I heard it done before. If I am being honest, I will still catch myself from time to time saying a phrase that I just heard prayed as a kid.

The point of all of this is that God wants to hear the heart, not just a "perfect prayer." His desire is relational. When I hear the word "empty," I think it really sums up the aspect of prayer that God does not want. He does not want us to just go through the motions. He does not want the conversation to be empty. He wants to know the depth of our thoughts in our prayer. He wants to know the heart behind what we desire. Do we desire our own selfish motives or are we genuinely caring and putting others before ourselves when we pray?

THINKING YOU ARE HEARD
DEVOTION #3 - PASTOR JOHN CARTER

"And when you pray, do not heap up empty phrases as the Gentiles do, for they think that they will be heard for their many words." Matthew 6:7

Yesterday, we looked at the first part of this verse. Today we are going to look at the later part of this verse. We walked through the idea of praying empty words or words of ritual and how God does not desire us to pray in this manner. The latter part of this verse expounds on that idea, *"They think they will be heard for their many words."* In your mind, what do you think of when you consider that last phrase?

I cannot help but think of a church potluck. When I was a growing boy, I was always hungry. I would go to grab a plate and then someone would say, "Hey, let us pray before we eat." As I scanned the room, I would just beg that no one call on "Bob." I wanted anybody but Bob (Bob is a fictional character, but you will get my point). Sure enough, Bob was called on to pray for the blessing on the meal and 45 mins later, with a full sermon along with an altar call, we finally get to eating a meal. What could have been a simple, "Jesus, thank you for this food! Amen," turned into a full-on dissertation of the end times or whatever was preached prior to the potluck. I can literally remember thinking, "Did not we just have a church message; why are we doing this again?" I do not know if this resembles something you may have experienced in your life. It probably felt longer than it actually was because I was really hungry. I get that, in the mind of a hungry child, what was probably just five minutes, just extended out to feel like 45 minutes.

I cannot help but think that sometimes we do this as adults as well. The aspect of being patient when we pray is not often talked about. Just as impatient as I was to eat when the prayer was horribly long-winded, we as adults can find ourselves in the same boat as the hungry child. When we really need something and we pray earnestly over and over again the same prayer, we can be uncertain if God even hears us. So, we do it again just to make sure He got the memo. It becomes the "little hungry boy that wants to eat" syndrome just in adult form. Sometimes, it even gets us to start doubting God Himself. Since it seems God is not answering me, He did not hear me; therefore, He must not care about me. He must be angry with me. We can wonder, "Is God even real?"

Solomon wrote these words in Ecclesiastes 5:2, *"Be not rash with your mouth, nor let your heart be hasty to utter a word before God, for God is in heaven and you are on earth. Therefore let your words be few."*

It is said a little differently in Proverbs 10:19, *"When words are many, transgression is not lacking, but whoever restrains his lips is prudent."*

This is not saying not to pray. This is saying to be intentional about what you are praying for or what you are praying about. Asking God to give you a new car so you can be cool is a little different than asking God to heal a broken aspect of your life. Matthew 6:7 is a verse that is leading up to a very serious aspect of prayer and petitioning God. Take some time and consider the things you pray for.

A GOD THAT KNOWS

DEVOTION #4 - PASTOR JOHN CARTER

"Do not be like them, for your Father knows what you need before you ask him." Matthew 6:8

I am going to break this passage up into two aspects of thought. The first aspect is that the Father is God and God knows everything. The second aspect, which we will dive deeper into tomorrow, is the fact that God is identified as our Father that cares. Today's title should give you an idea of the first aspect; it is the characteristic of God that He knows everything!

Consider that for a second and let it sink to your core. God knows everything! He knows your good and bad thoughts. He knows your good and bad deeds. He knows when we are faking it, and when we are not. He knows what you need versus what you want. He knows what is on your heart. He knows what burdens you are carrying now.

Have you ever had a conversation with someone who knew you so well that they understood where you were going in the conversation and could complete the thought for you? That is God, but in a completely amplified and intimate way. God not only knows the words, thoughts, and ideas, but He also knows the hurt, pain, and emotion that is connected to the words. He knows the difference between the face we put on for others and the authentic person we are on the inside.

I like how David puts it in Psalm 38:9, *"O Lord, all my longing is before you; my sighing is not hidden from you."*

God knows when we are not okay; therefore, we do not have to pretend with Him. We can just be real and genuine.

In Psalm 69:17-20, David writes again about God's character and that He knows it all, *"Hide not your face from your servant, for I am in distress; make haste to answer me. Draw near to my soul, redeem me; ransom me because of my enemies! You know my reproach, and my shame and my dishonor; my foes are all known to you. Reproaches have broken my heart, so that I am in despair. I looked for pity, but there was none, and for comforters, but I found none."*

Psalm 69:32-33 continues, *"When the humble see it they will be glad; you who seek God, let your hearts revive. For the Lord hears the needy and does not despise his own people who are prisoners."*

In this Psalm, David is walking through the aspects of sin that God knows. David does not hide the fact that there is sin in his life that brings shame, dishonor, and reproach.

Today, we are coming to grips with the fact that God knows, and I mean He *knows* everything. Take some time and really approach Him with that at the forefront of your prayers. This might mean you need to acknowledge some areas of shame, dishonor, and reproach. Confess these things to God and ask Him to help you not walk in sin. It could mean that you just need to let some things go and pour your burdens out to God. It is not like He does not know you are carrying them. It may be a deep longing you have that you desperately need to ask God to help you with. Please realize that He knows that longing exists already, so share it with Him.

In all the things we approach God with, our needs, wants, desires, and confessions, it is always important to realize that God knows our hearts. He knows our intent. The best way to approach Him is to be honest and be willing to take the instruction He gives you as the best thing for you. Let me leave you with this passage from Hebrews 12:10, *"For they [earthly fathers] disciplined us for a short time as it seemed best to them, but he [heavenly Father] disciplines us for our good, that we may share his holiness."*

A FATHER THAT CARES

DEVOTION #5 - PASTOR JOHN CARTER

"Do not be like them, for your Father knows what you need before you ask him." Matthew 6:8

Yesterday, we walked through the fact that God knows everything. We considered how that might change the way we approach God. Today, we are going to focus on God being our Father.

I am going to be real with you. Just the mentioning of a father might send you off into "bad memory land." You may have never had a father that reflected the kindness of the Father God. It is really hard to correlate God as a Father when your earthly father was, well, not great. Maybe your earthly father was absent, not loving, or maybe even straight-up abusive. This is why it is so important to dive into the many passages that talk about God as an amazing and loving Father. When we confess Jesus as our Lord and Savior, it is automatic. God is our Father.

Paul links a lot of Old Testament ideas into this simple, yet profound, verse found in 2 Corinthians 6:18, *"And I will be a father to you, and you shall be sons and daughters to me, says the Lord Almighty."*

John says it this way in 1 John 3:1-3, *"See what kind of love the Father has given to us, that we should be called children of God; and so we are. The reason why the world does not know us is that it did not know him. Beloved, we are God's children now, and what we will be has not yet appeared; but we know that when he appears we shall be like him, because we shall see him as he is. And everyone who thus hopes in him purifies himself as he is pure."*

Our hope in Christ means that there is an element in our life that has to change and be conformed to mirror the likeness of Christ. John puts it in terms of purifying ourselves like Jesus.

In Matthew 7:9-11, it is described this way, *"Or which one of you, if his son asks him for bread, will give him a stone? Or if he asks for a fish, will give him a serpent? If you then, who are evil, know how to give good gifts to your children, how much more will your Father who is in heaven give good things to those who ask him!"* Ultimately, there are so many other verses I could have you read about the goodness and love of our Heavenly Father.

Maybe you have never prayed to God with this as a consideration. God is someone we can approach like a loving, kind, and caring father. I think 1 Peter 5:6-7 fits in so well here, *"Humble yourselves, therefore, under the mighty hand of God so that at the proper time he may exalt you, casting all your anxieties on him, because he cares for you."*

It literally says here in the Bible that God cares for you!

Today, take that with you everywhere you go. It is powerful to realize that an all-knowing, all-powerful God is your Father and He genuinely and authentically cares for you. When you talk to Him today, give Him a big, huge hug. Let Him know how much you love Him, too.

NEEDS VS. WANTS
DEVOTION #6 - PASTOR JOHN CARTER

As we conclude this week's devotions and go into gathering together with the saints, I want to conclude the study of Matthew 6:7-8 with this difficult introspection of needs versus wants.

Jesus is about to walk us through a model prayer. He has just set up many different dos and do nots for us to consider when looking into prayer.

1. Do not pray for others to see or recognize us.
2. Do not pray with large eloquent words.
3. Do not pray over and over again in hopes of being heard.
4. Do pray in secret and praying intimately.
5. Do pray knowing we have a God who knows and a Father who cares.

These are some of the things we have covered through our devotions in the last couple of weeks. I love that Jesus, as the instructor in this passage of Matthew chapter 6, informs us that our needs are clearly known to our Heavenly Father. Often times, it is when our wants are not met that we seem to get frustrated. Many say, "Yeah, all my needs are met, but I really want _____!" Have you ever fallen for this trap of the devil? I know I have. You see this happens to me when I shift my mind from a grateful heart, to the irritating little brat that thinks all my wants should be answered like my needs.

Has this ever happened to you? Have you mixed your needs and your wants all up? It is really a matter of priority, at least for me it is. I usually find myself full of stress because my wants are not being met and I give no thought to my needs. Ironically, they are being met. Examine today what you are stressing about. Is it a need or is it a want? When I am in one of these fits, as soon as I walk through the needs vs. wants and realize I am mostly stressing over wants, I quickly find myself thanking God that He has supplied my needs. It changes my approach to prayer and adoration to God from one that is full of stress to one that is full of gratitude.

In Matthew chapter 6, towards the end of the chapter, Jesus walks us through anxiety and the things we ought not to stress over. Matthew 6:25-26 says, *"Therefore I tell you, do not be anxious about your life, what you will eat or what you will drink, nor about your body, what you will put on. Is not life more than food, and the body more than clothing? Look at the birds of the air: they neither sow nor reap nor gather into barns, and yet your heavenly Father feeds them. Are you not of more value than they?"*

Jesus goes into more detail about the lilies of the valley and how they are covered with more splendor than Solomon. Matthew 6:31-33 adds, *"Therefore do not be anxious, saying, 'What shall we eat?' or 'What shall we drink?' or 'What shall we wear?' For the Gentiles seek after all these things, and your heavenly Father knows that you need them all. But seek first the kingdom of God and his righteousness, and all these things will be added to you."*

The call is that we not get distracted with all the needs and wants of life, but to be sure we have truly sought after the most important thing of all, the Kingdom of God and His righteousness. Today, as you are examining your prayer life and what that might mean for you, let me draw your attention back to Jesus' words. Seek Him, His Kingdom, and His righteousness.

Paul says a very similar thing in Philippians 4:4-7, *"Rejoice in the Lord always; again I will say, rejoice. Let your reasonableness be known to everyone. The Lord is at hand; do not be anxious about anything, but in everything by prayer and supplication with thanksgiving let your requests be made known to God. And the peace of God, which surpasses all understanding, will guard your hearts and your minds in Christ Jesus."*

Let me challenge you to simply take everything we have talked about so far and just do it.

- Know that God hears us when we pray.
- God knows what we need.
- He cares about us.
- He wants us to make His kingdom our priority.
- He wants us to pursue His righteousness in our life.

Today, rest in the person of Jesus and anchor yourself to His promises. Take some time to just seek Him and praise Him for who He is.

The Lord's Prayer
Part I

PASTOR CHUCK LINDSEY

"In this manner, therefore, pray: Our Father in heaven, Hallowed be Your name. Your kingdom come. Your will be done on earth as it is in heaven." Matthew 6:9-10 (NKJV)

In verse 9, Jesus moves from assuring us that God hears us, to teaching us how to actually do it. He is teaching us how to **"pray."** We will break this prayer up, very naturally, into two sections. The first (verses 9-10) is focused on God. The second (verses 11-13) is focused on our needs.

This prayer is often, mistakenly, called the "Lord's Prayer." It is not the Lord Jesus' prayer. His prayer is in John chapter 17. This is the Lord teaching us how to pray.

1. At what age did you first hear of this prayer? Did you memorize it?

_____

_____

_____

2. What could be a better name for this prayer?

_____

_____

_____

I want to begin with the word **"pray."** **"Pray"** is from the Greek verb "proseuchomai" and it means to "petition, or to ask." The word comes from two Greek words that mean "to ask for" and "favorable towards." It is the idea that you are asking God to be favorable towards you and your need, or towards what you are asking Him to do. This means, perhaps obviously, that prayer is fundamentally going to God in need. It is asking Him to not only notice our need (this is what Jesus already assured us of), but it is asking Him to step in and help. It is in this way that we see one of the many benefits of prayer; it puts us in the right relation to God.

3. What are some other benefits of prayer?

_____

_____

_____

4. What does it mean to be in the right relation to God?

_____

_____

_____

What do I mean? I mean that prayer places us under God, in need of Him. Real prayer solves one of man's greatest problems. Humanity's problem has always been the same. We exalt ourselves above God! We have done this since the very beginning. Back in the garden, Adam and Eve did not just eat fruit, they exalted themselves and their desires above God and what He wanted. They denied Him and chose themselves! In so doing, they unknowingly followed the example of the serpent who enticed them. Isaiah chapter 14 tells us that Satan exalted himself above God, *"For you have said in your heart: 'I will ascend into heaven, I will exalt my throne above the stars of God. I will also sit on the mount of the congregation on the farthest sides of the north; I will ascend above the heights of the clouds, I will be like the Most High'"* (Isaiah 14:13-14, NKJV). Adam and Eve, and every person since, have done the same thing. Prayer fixes this. It is intrinsically humbling. It places us under God, looking up to Him in need, as a young child to their father. We need prayer.

5. Explain how prayer can be affected by pride.

_____

_____

_____

Now that we understand the place prayer puts us in, we can begin to ask correctly. Jesus says **"pray"** like this. What follows is something of a roadmap, a template, or a format for prayer. First, there is a warning. This is not designed to be rehearsed and recited. Jesus was not telling us, "These are the specific words you use." It is not wrong to memorize this prayer, but Jesus was not giving us a script. He was teaching us a "formula" if you will, a structure to prayer. You will see it as we go; but it is not the specific words, it is the focus behind those words that Jesus is teaching.

6. What are some of the elements you notice in this prayer?

_____

_____

_____

First, He says **"<u>pray</u>"** to your **_"Father."_** This means to begin in prayer with the recognition that the One you are speaking to, who is God, is also your Father who loves you. So again, the words "our Father" are not required at the beginning of every prayer. It is the recognition of who we are speaking to that is needed. I do this. Before I begin to pray (publicly or privately), I always pause to recognize who I am talking to. It is my Dad who loves me.

7. Is it okay to pray to Jesus? The Holy Spirit? Mary? A deceased relative?

[handwritten notes]: examples — God (Father) bless Son (brother + sisters) — Holy Spirit — Act 7:59, Jude 20 — John 13:14 — Eph 6:18 — John 14:13-14 — John 16:23 — John 15:16 — Hebrews 4:14-16

Next, is the recognition that God is above us and holy. Jesus says, "Our Father who is in heaven, hallowed is Your name." **_"Hallowed"_** comes from the Greek word "hagiazo" and means "to be separate, set apart."

In this word is the recognition that there is no one like the Lord. He is infinitely above and beyond all. Everything else has been created, He alone is eternal. Everything else is limited; He is limitless, all-knowing, and all-powerful. He "alone is God and besides Him there is no other" (Deuteronomy 4:35). From first recognizing Him as our loving Father, we then stop to remember that He is God, that He is holy, and that He is above and beyond all things. Here again, we are placed in our right position beneath Him, looking up to the One who is God and who loves us.

8. What are some other words that could be used to open prayer while recognizing the greatness of God?

_____

_____

_____

From here we are to remind ourselves that this Earth is not all there is. Verse 10 reminds us that a true *"Kingdom"* exists and is **coming**. **"Coming"** is from the Greek word "erchmai" and means "to come to be."

His *"Kingdom"* will one day come and overtake the "kingdoms" of this Earth (Daniel 2). This coming Kingdom is His. It is a Kingdom that will endure forever and where He will rule and reign as King always. The prayer here, for this *"kingdom come,"* is a prayer asking for His ways and His will to become reality in my life. It is a prayer to our King to bring His ways into our life, marriage, family, parenting, pursuits, and desires. Make no mistake, His kingdom will come one day to this Earth, but before it does, it is meant to come into our lives individually. Every believer's life is meant to be a display of His Kingdom! It is a place where Jesus rules as King, His ways are our ways, His will is our will, and His work is our mission. In the same way, we read the words *"Your will be done."*

9. What does it mean that His Kingdom is meant to come into our lives individually?

_____

_____

_____

"Done" comes from the Greek word "ginomai" and it means "to be brought into."

This is a prayer that asks for what He wants to be accomplished in our lives. It is saying, "Dad, I want what you want. What you want is always best. Have Your way in my life." At the end of the day, these are prayers for growth. It is asking Him to grow us, change us, and make us different people. It is asking for our lives to be what He wants them to be. It is asking for Him to make us like Him. This is a request He always answers.

10. Have you prayed this prayer? When?

_____

_____

_____

Now, in terms of our prayer "roadmap," verses 9 and 10 have us looking up, reminding ourselves who He is and what He wants. In the next chapter, we will look at verses 11-13 where we are told to bow our heads to ask for our needs and the needs of others. It is in this way that Jesus is giving us a pattern in prayer. The order is:

- Look up before you look around.
- Worship before you ask.
- Remind before you request.

It means to pause before we ask for anything to remind ourselves who we are talking to. Then, we are to let who He is fill our hearts and flood into our circumstances to bring us to a place of worship.

Jesus would say, "So, pray like this: I stop to recognize that you are both my Father and God. You love me and are supremely holy. May your ways become my ways in everything."

NOTES

LOVING GOD

DEVOTION #1 - PASTOR JOHN CARTER

"'Teacher, which is the great commandment in the Law?' And he said to him, 'You shall love the Lord your God with all your heart and with all your soul and with all your mind. This is the great and first commandment. And a second is like it: You shall love your neighbor as yourself.'" Matthew 22:36-39

This is a famously quoted passage of Scripture in the church. It may be news to some of you that Matthew is not where this originated from. Jesus, being the Living Word of God (John 1:1), is not afraid to point us back to the very powerful words of God in the Old Testament. In fact, you will find Jesus often referencing the teachings of Moses and the prophets in the New Testament.

Deuteronomy 6:5-7 is where the greatest commandment is first written down in Scripture, *"You shall love the Lord your God with all your heart and with all your soul and with all your might. And these words that I command you today shall be on your heart. You shall teach them diligently to your children, and shall talk of them when you sit in your house, and when you walk by the way, and when you lie down, and when you rise."*

As we get ready to walk through the Lord's Prayer, we are going to focus on two parts in the same way Jesus does in teaching us this manner in which we are to pray. This week, we will focus on when we pray in a manner that shows the Father how much we love Him, He is honored, worshiped, and revered as the God that He is in our life. This love of ours is going to be limited in comparison to the love the Father has for us, but as Scripture shows us, we are to demonstrate our love to the Father in a manner that involves all of our being - heart, soul, and mind. This is the greatest commandment given to the children of God, to love Him with all of our person.

Consider the word *"all."* Have you ever considered what it would look like if you gave God all of you? Do you hold back in certain areas? How about the not-so-pretty areas or the areas we are ashamed of? I love that this commandment originates in the Old Testament because it shows me God's expectation of worship has not changed. He desires that the church would worship Him in the same manner the Israelites did, with all of their person and being.

We are going to examine Matthew 6:9-10. It is known as the Lord's Prayer. One thing you will see quickly is that the prayer begins with this understanding that it is all about God! He is first and primary! He is who is to be adored, worshiped, honored, feared, and reverenced.

Matthew 6:9-10 says, *"Pray then like this: 'Our Father in heaven, hallowed be your name. Your kingdom come, your will be done, on earth as it is in heaven.'"*

Consider this as you are going about your day, "How do I worship God in prayer with all of my being or person - heart, soul, and mind?" I hope you are looking forward to diving deep into the things Jesus teaches us about prayer and how to do it in a way that pleases the Father.

It is going to be important to understand this about Jesus' example of prayer; He is not saying pray in a ritualistic manner and just repeat these words after me. Every line of the prayer has a deep and impactful meaning to how we recognize who God is in our life. We will walk through these each day adding depth to the way we approach God, our Father.

The ultimate goal at the end of this is to know how to love God with all our being and person and be able to express that love in the facet of prayer.

FATHER'S HOLY NAME

DEVOTION #2 - PASTOR JOHN CARTER

"Pray then like this: 'Our Father in heaven, hallowed be your name.'" Matthew 6:9

I think before I dive into this passage, I should make sure the context has been set for this verse. If you have not been following along, we have been walking through how not to pray. Jesus laid down the "do not pray like" this section first and now He is taking us through the "to-do" section. It is easy to ignore the do not and only look at the do. As a society, being told not to do something comes across as offensive and overbearing. Understand that Jesus found both to be absolutely relevant. He starts this verse with the very statement to pray *"like this."* The key word is *"like."* He did not say pray exactly these words but like this. So, if you have not examined the Ways Jesus has told us not to pray, then may I encourage you to just look back a couple of verses and read what Jesus says. Then, dive into following what He says to do.

The opening statement is very profound in this example of prayer Jesus sets before us. *"Our Father"* emphasizes that we are going before the comfort of a loving Father and it brings immense adoration to our prayer.

Psalm 103 is amazing. I encourage you to read the whole chapter. It goes right along with what Jesus is teaching in Matthew. Psalm 103:1 says, *"Bless the Lord, O my soul, and all that is within me, bless his holy name!"* Psalm 103:4 adds, *"Who redeems your life from the pit, who crowns you with steadfast love and mercy?"* Psalm 103:10-12 says, *"He does not deal with us according to our sins, nor repay us according to our iniquities. For as high as the heavens are above the earth, so great is his steadfast love toward those who fear him; as far as the east is from the west, so far does he remove our transgressions from us."* Those last words are so beautiful. Psalm 103:13-14 says, *"As a father shows compassion to his children, so the Lord shows compassion to those who fear him. For he knows our frame; he remembers that we are dust."* Psalm 103:17-18 adds, *"But the steadfast love of the Lord is from everlasting to everlasting on those who fear him, and his righteousness to children's children, to those who keep his covenant and remember to do his commandments."*

Seriously, take time today and read Psalm 103; it will definitely be worth your time.

Jesus points us to this amazing love that we have in the Father and wants us to understand this first and foremost when we come before Him to pray. Even when we are praying to ask God for forgiveness from our sins and our iniquities, there is this promise that God, like a compassionate father, will be compassionate towards us.

The other element Jesus points us to is the Name of God. Not only is His name *"Father,"* but He is in every aspect superior to anything or anyone else.

In the phrase, *"hallowed be your name,"* Jesus approaches God with the intimacy of a father, but also with reverence and fear of One whose very name is Holy. Think through that for a second. Name one thing in your mind that you would consider so holy that you dare not even evoke its very name. You may find yourself struggling to even identify something holy outside of God. Holiness has left our society, and even in some sense, our churches. We struggle to really grasp and understand the word "holy" because our minds cannot even fathom what it is supposed to be.

With holy water, holy or sacred places, holy temple, and Holy Spirit, we have this word inundated with our Scripture but do we understand it? Can we define it? When Jesus says, *"hallowed be your name,"* He is saying, "God let your name continue to be holy, or may it be kept holy (by your people); may your name be treated with almighty reverence."

Isaiah puts it like this in Isaiah 29:22-24, ***"Therefore thus says the Lord, who redeemed Abraham, concerning the house of Jacob: 'Jacob shall no more be ashamed, no more shall his face grow pale. For when he sees his children, the work of my hands, in his midst, they will sanctify my name; they will sanctify the Holy One of Jacob and will stand in awe of the God of Israel. And those who go astray in spirit will come to understanding, and those who murmur will accept instruction.'"***

God's name is not meant to be treated as a common name, but as a name of distinct reverence and awe. Jesus wants to teach us that we get to have this amazing intimate relationship with a father, but we must not forget that God has holiness about Him that we ought to be aware of when we walk in His presence.

There is so much to unpack in just this one line. Take some time today to Google the names of God the Father and look at some of the names that surround our Father's character. Some that stick out to me are these:

- El Roi = the God who sees me
- YHWH-Raah = God my shepherd
- YHWH-Rapha = God that heals me
- YHWH-Mekoddishkem = God who sanctifies me
- YHWH-Jireh = God our provider
- YHWH-Shalom = God our peace
- Adonai = True Lord and Master

Isaiah 9:6 has some great names of our Father as well.

We truly have an amazing opportunity when we pray. We are able to go before our Father and talk with Him. Please remember some of these holy attributes and make sure we recognize His holy awesomeness!

POWERFUL KINGDOM
DEVOTION #3 - PASTOR JOHN CARTER

"Your kingdom come, your will be done, on earth as it is in heaven." Matthew 6:10

Today, we are only going to focus on three words, *"your kingdom come."*

As I stated in previous devotions, Jesus is teaching us some absolutely amazing concepts of how we are to approach the Father God in prayer. Each line of the Lord's Prayer is packed with immensely deep and practical truth that is so hard to unpack in one devotion.

What is the first thing you think of when you consider a kingdom? Some things that come to my mind are that there is a king, the kingdom covers a vast amount of area, and there is an army that enforces the rules or laws. Outside of that, I really do not know that I have a great mental picture of a kingdom. In America, we do not really see our land as a kingdom, so it just does not correlate. I can envision what Hollywood has created as these great kingdoms do battle in movies like *"The Hobbit."* Maybe those are good images of what a kingdom looks like. So, when Jesus says, *"your kingdom come,"* what is he trying to teach us in prayer?

In 1 John 5:18-19, we read, *"We know that everyone who has been born of God does not keep on sinning, but he who was born of God protects him, and the evil one does not touch him. We know that we are from God, and the whole world lies in the power of the evil one."*

I think it is important to first understand that we are living in a world that is ruled by the kingdom of darkness. The world is under the power of the evil one. So when Jesus is saying, *"your kingdom come,"* He knows and is teaching us that we ought to be desiring the return and the presence of God. He is teaching us that when we pray, we ought to be focused and concerned with our own hearts being ready to be with God. We ought not to love the wickedness of the world, but we should be longing to be under the rule and reign of a holy and righteous God.

I want to share with you some prophecies about this Kingdom of God that we are being taught to desire and pray will come.

In Daniel, we see the interpretation of an earthly king's dream. In that interpretation, there is a prophecy of the future Kingdom of God. Daniel 2:44-45 says, *"And in the days of those kings the God of heaven will set up a kingdom that shall never be destroyed, nor shall the kingdom be left to another people. It shall break in pieces all these kingdoms and bring them to an end, and it shall stand forever, just as you saw that a stone was cut from a mountain by no human hand, and that it broke in pieces the iron, the bronze, the clay, the silver, and the gold. A great God has made known to the king what shall be after this. The dream is certain, and its interpretation sure."*

Isaiah describes it like this in Isaiah 2:2-3, *"It shall come to pass in the latter days that the mountain of the house of the Lord shall be established as the highest of the mountains, and shall be lifted up above the hills; and all the nations shall flow to it, and many peoples shall come, and say: 'Come, let us go up to the mountain of the Lord, to the house of the God of Jacob, that he may teach us his ways and that we may walk in his paths.' For out of Zion shall go forth the law, and the word of the Lord from Jerusalem."*

Jeremiah articulates it like this in Jeremiah 23:5-6, *"Behold, the days are coming, declares the Lord, when I will raise up for David a righteous Branch, and he shall reign as king and deal wisely, and shall execute justice and righteousness in the land. In his days Judah will be saved, and Israel will dwell securely.*

And this is the name by which he will be called: 'The Lord is our righteousness.'"

The Kingdom of Heaven is not some imaginary fantasy. There is a King. There are ways which this Kingdom will operate. This Kingdom will destroy all the earthly kingdoms that operate under the rule of the evil one.

When Jesus is teaching us to pray, He is asking us to recognize the future King. He is the Ruler of the Kingdom that will last forever. Remember the greatest commandment is to love the Lord with all your heart, soul, and mind. Part of this means that we are to desire His righteous ruling of this Earth.

Your Kingdom come!

AUTHORITY TO ACCOMPLISH

DEVOTION #4 - PASTOR JOHN CARTER

"Your kingdom come, your will be done, on earth as it is in heaven." Matthew 6:10

Today we are going to walk through four words, *"your will be done."* Putting these instructions that Jesus gives us about prayer into practice is going to be very hard. Honestly, most of the time when we approach God in prayer, it is usually because we want to convince God to act on our behalf. I am just as guilty of this as anyone. Jesus is pointing us to the very aspect of prayer that is so critical; we need to be willing to walk in the will of God.

The line in this verse, ultimately, is showing us Who has authority and power in our life. It is not just some authority or power but all authority and power. It is *"your will be done."*

Meditate on those words for a second and consider your prayer life. Is there a semblance of God's will at the forefront of your conversation? Our prayers could begin with, "God, I do not like pain and I do not want heartache. I want what is best for my life and no one knows what the best thing for my life is but You. So, whatever Your will is, I am in!"

This is probably one of the hardest realities of prayer that we need to come to grips with. It seems so much on the opposite spectrum of what prayer is. If prayer is just an avenue to tell God how we want things to be, then this concept is definitely going to feel, taste, and sound like insanity. Our mindset should be that regardless of the outcome, regardless of the result, if it goes the way I want or not, God I desire your will above anything else!

Can I actually pray that and have it be genuine and real? Can I trust God with my kids, wife, work, and life? Can I trust Him to really be the God that promises He will never leave me or forsake me? Can I trust Him to be my shelter and place of refuge? Can I trust God to be my rest, my shield from fiery arrows, and my strength? Can I trust Him to be my comfort, encouragement, and hope? I can go on and on with these questions. Hopefully, you will see that these questions encompass all of one's being. Think this through when you are confronted with the question, "Can I put my all in the hands of God?" Under those conditions, I need we need to say, *"Your will be done!"* If you are anything like me, there are probably areas in your life where you still feel like you need to dictate to God the way it should be done. It is probably a major source of stress and anxiety for you. I know it is hard for me. Maybe today you can take that particular area of your life and say to God, our Father, *"Your will be done."*

Hebrews 13:20-21 says, *"Now may the God of peace who brought again from the dead our Lord Jesus, the great shepherd of the sheep, by the blood of the eternal covenant, equip you with everything good that you may do his will, working in us that which is pleasing in his sight, through Jesus Christ, to whom be glory forever and ever. Amen."*

As Jesus is teaching us how to pray in Matthew chapter 6, this part of the lesson is a very critical aspect of His teaching. It is our will versus God's will. Which one is the most important to you? This is something that can easily cause us to dig even deeper, not just in aspects of prayer. Are we walking in areas that are contrary to the Lord? Have we surrendered every area of our life to the mighty, awesome God, who desires the love and adoration of His children? He wants all of our heart, soul, and mind!

Take some time today to ask God to show you the areas in your life you are still clinging to. Maybe, ask God to show you where you are insisting on your own will and not God's will. Be prepared and know the answer the Lord shows you may not be easy. I hope and pray today was an encouraging and edifying devotion. I am going to leave you with a passage from Proverbs 2:1-5, *"My son, if you receive my words and treasure up my commandments with you, making your ear attentive to wisdom and inclining your heart to understanding; yes, if you call out for insight and raise your voice for understanding, if you seek it like silver and search for it as for hidden treasures, then you will understand the fear of the Lord and find the knowledge of God."*

REALM OF AUTHORITY
DEVOTION #5 - PASTOR JOHN CARTER

"Your kingdom come, your will be done, on earth as it is in heaven." Matthew 6:10

"On earth as it is in heaven" is where we are going to focus our attention today. As we have been walking through Jesus' instructions on how to pray, we have spent time looking at how not to pray. This week, we started with how to pray. In the first few lines of the model prayer, Jesus has pointed us completely to the person and being of God the Father. I believe this is Jesus' way of showing us how, in our prayers, to keep the first and greatest commandment to love God with all our heart, soul, and mind at the forefront. Yesterday, we talked about God's authority in our life and whether He can indeed be trusted with every aspect of our life. Today, we are going to hopefully expand that trust beyond our realm of comprehension.

This simple phrase, *"on earth as it is in Heaven,"* has such a massive, powerful, and hopefully encouraging implication to the children of God. As we wrestle with following our own will versus the will of God, we may still be working through full submission to God. This line in the prayer Jesus gives us is so profound.

Let me ask you to write down all the things you think you control. If you are a parent, you might say you are in control of your house and family. If you are a business owner, you may say you have your business under control. Those are just two examples and if you have been in either of those positions for any length of time, you understand that control is a fleeting word in those dynamics. In a matter of seconds, things can easily spin out of control and soon you begin to question what it was you actually thought you were in control of. This is going to be a bit of a mental stretch, but expand that thought to the whole world. Jesus is still pointing us to the amazing and unfathomable control God has. He has complete control of Heaven the way it runs and operates and is structured. The sun's rising and the setting of the stars are all prostrated by the very will of God. I think of what King Nebuchadnezzar said when his mind and reason came back to him.

Daniel 4:34-35 records, *"At the end of the days I, Nebuchadnezzar, lifted my eyes to heaven, and my reason returned to me, and I blessed the Most High, and praised and honored him who lives forever, for his dominion is an everlasting dominion, and his kingdom endures from generation to generation; all the inhabitants of the earth are accounted as nothing, and he does according to his will among the host of heaven and among the inhabitants of the earth; and none can stay his hand or say to him, 'What have you done?'"*

Psalm 103:20-21 adds, *"Bless the Lord, O you his angels, you mighty ones who do his word, obeying the voice of his word! Bless the Lord, all his hosts, his ministers, who do his will!"*

These are just a few passages that expound on the fact that the heavenly hosts and all that is in Heaven, obey the Father and that the Father is in control. God's authority is not limited to just a heavenly realm. He has authority in our earthly realm all the same. It is, *"Your will be done, on earth as it is in Heaven."*

Maybe you are struggling to know the will of God. Maybe it is not something that you have ever even considered. The Bible is not super mysterious about God's will. He tells us all throughout Scripture what His will is. Most of the time we just do not want to hear it. We choose our way over God's way and so we walk our own path instead of what God has for us. Think about that for a second. If I am being honest, I can barely keep my family in control. Running a business consumed me. Yet I want to, in my pride, put up my understanding against the guy (God) who controls and operates the Heavens and the Earth. It sounds silly because it is silly! So often this is what we are saying by our actions and decisions we make every day. The Bible is full of verses that clearly tell us His will.

- *"I delight to do your will, O my God; your law is within my heart."* Psalm 40:8

- *"And this is the will of him who sent me, that I should lose nothing of all that he has given me, but raise it up on the last day. For this is the will of my Father, that everyone who looks on the Son and believes in him should have eternal life, and I will raise him up on the last day."* John 6:39-40

- *"And when he had removed him, he raised up David to be their king, of whom he testified and said, 'I have found in David the son of Jesse a man after my heart, who will do all my will.'"* Acts 13:22

- *"And he said, 'The God of our fathers appointed you to know his will, to see the Righteous One and to hear a voice from his mouth; for you will be a witness for him to everyone of what you have seen and heard. And now why do you wait? Rise and be baptized and wash away your sins, calling on his name.'"* Acts 22:14-16

- *"Do not be conformed to this world, but be transformed by the renewal of your mind, that by testing you may discern what is the will of God, what is good and acceptable and perfect."* Romans 12:2

- *"Bondservants, obey your earthly masters with fear and trembling, with a sincere heart, as you would Christ, not by the way of eye-service, as people-pleasers, but as bondservants of Christ, doing the will of God from the heart, rendering service with a good will as to the Lord and not to man, knowing that whatever good anyone does, this he will receive back from the Lord, whether he is a bondservant or is free."* Ephesians 6:5-8

- *"For this is the will of God, your sanctification: that you abstain from sexual immorality; that each one of you know how to control his own body in holiness and honor, not in the passion of lust like the Gentiles who do not know God; that no one transgress and wrong his brother in this matter, because the Lord is an avenger in all these things, as we told you beforehand and solemnly warned you. For God has not called us for impurity, but in holiness."* 1 Thessalonians 4:3-7

- *"For this is the will of God, that by doing good you should put to silence the ignorance of foolish people."* 1 Peter 2:15

- *"Since therefore Christ suffered in the flesh, arm yourselves with the same way of thinking, for whoever has suffered in the flesh has ceased from sin, so as to live for the rest of the time in the flesh no longer for human passions but for the will of God."* 1 Peter 4:1-2

I could go on and on with verses that show us the will of God for us. My point is that it is not a mystery. We need to diligently seek it and pursue it. Pray for it! *"Your will be done, on earth as it is in heaven"* is the mindset we must have when we approach God. Do we seek and desire His will to be done today?

In 2 Corinthians 6:1-2, we read, *"Working together with him, then, we appeal to you not to receive the grace of God in vain. For he says, 'In a favorable time I listened to you, and in a day of salvation I have helped you.' Behold, now is the favorable time; behold, now is the day of salvation."*

SUMMARY OF REVERANCE
DEVOTION #6 - PASTOR JOHN CARTER

"Do not be like them, for your Father knows what you need before you ask him. Pray then like this: 'Our Father in heaven, hallowed be your name. Your kingdom come, your will be done, on earth as it is in heaven.'" Matthew 6:8-10

As we conclude our week on Matthew 6:9-10, we are just going to reminisce about the awesome things Jesus taught us about prayer. Ultimately, I see Jesus pointing us back to the holy reverence that God deserves. From His holy name, His powerful Kingdom, His majestic will, to His mighty realm of authority, it all points to a God that is able. That is something worth getting excited about! That is something worth praising God about! Tomorrow is Sunday and the church is gathering together to worship God. We hope to see you there.

Today, I want you to rest on several things. You can rest in the fact that God knows where you are in life. He knows it all! He knows the things you are struggling with, and the desires or dreams you have yet to accomplish. Rest in the amazing, saving grace that God has given us through his Son, Jesus. Rest in His mercy. Revel in His person, character, power, and will. Take time today to just be with God.

Here are some verses to encourage you in this aspect of rest that God wants us to enjoy.

- *"Come to me, all who labor and are heavy laden, and I will give you rest. Take my yoke upon you, and learn from me, for I am gentle and lowly in heart, and you will find rest for your souls. For my yoke is easy, and my burden is light."* Matthew 11:28-30

- *"So then, there remains a Sabbath rest for the people of God, for whoever has entered God's rest has also rested from his works as God did from his. Let us therefore strive to enter that rest, so that no one may fall by the same sort of disobedience."* Hebrews 4:9-11

- *"The Lord is my shepherd; I shall not want. He makes me lie down in green pastures. He leads me beside still waters. He restores my soul. He leads me in paths of righteousness for his name's sake. Even though I walk through the valley of the shadow of death, I will fear no evil, for you are with me; your rod and your staff, they comfort me. You prepare a table before me in the presence of my enemies; you anoint my head with oil; my cup overflows. Surely goodness and mercy shall follow me all the days of my life, and I shall dwell in the house of the Lord forever."* Psalm 23:1-6

I hope you find the amazing rest of Jesus Christ in your life. I pray that as we continue to walk through the many aspects of prayer, you will always come back to the amazing place of rest we have in Jesus. Life is hectic for sure and there are always multiple distractions happening all around us. Taking the time to just be in awe of who God is, what He has done for you, and all of His goodness and mercies, is very much what this week's study of prayer is all about. It is about God. It should always be about His character, Kingdom, desire, and purpose for us. Enjoy His amazing love and care for each and every one of us. Spend some time just thanking and worshiping God one-on-one! He loves His one-on-one time with His children. I hope you come away with a sense of awe and wonder. I pray you will see that God is ever present in your day as you grow even closer to Him.

LESSON FIVE

The Lord's Prayer Part II

PASTOR CHUCK LINDSEY

"Give us this day our daily bread. And forgive us our debts, as we forgive our debtors. And do not lead us into temptation, but deliver us from the evil one. For Yours is the kingdom and the power and the glory forever. Amen." Matthew 6:11-13 (NKJV)

We now come to the point where we ask. We have paused, we have looked up, and we have reminded ourselves who He is. We are now ready to ask.

The order here is important. Jesus told us to first look up, then ask. Remind yourself, then request. Doing this will dramatically affect what we ask for. I have so many times gone to God in prayer intending to ask Him for something or to do something specific only to have that radically change after I have paused to remind myself of who I am talking to. This is what prayer really is. Prayer is not trying to get God to do what we want Him to do. It is not begging Him to give in, as a child relentlessly begs for ice cream until the weary parent finally gives in to the incessant requests. No! Prayer is not trying to change God's mind or convince God to do something He does not want to do. It is not a cosmic religious arm-twisting! Prayer is all about alignment. It is the alignment of our hearts to His. It is like a radio. A radio must be tuned to the station so that music will come through. The radio does not make the music. It just picks up the music that is being broadcast. If it is tuned to the station properly, then it "reflects" what that station is playing. In the same way, true prayer is when my heart is tuned to the "station" of His heart and I begin to ask for what He is asking for. This is prayer. So we look up, "tune in" to the station if you will, and then we ask.

1. How can we know what God wants us to pray?

_____

_____

_____

The first word of this section is the word **"give." "Give"** comes from the Greek verb "didomi" and means "to give of one's own accord or desire, to bestow."

This is a request for God to *"give"* what only He can give. The word describes a gift that is given, simply because the giver wants to give it. Here again, our Lord is telling us who He is. He tells us to ask because He wants to give. Notice, the prayer here is for our daily needs, ***"Give us [because you want to!] this day our daily bread."*** This is not limited to bread, but rather refers to any regular and specific needs we might have. It is as easy as a request to give us the water we need to drink today, the money we need to pay those bills, or the strength to make that phone call.

2. Did you believe God wants to bless you?

_____

_____

_____

The words *"day"* and *"daily"* are important too. They are Jesus' way of saying, "Come to Me daily, continually." This is not a one-time "blanket" prayer, "God give me the work I need for the rest of my life. Amen!" This is, "Today Lord; sustain us today." It reminds me of what it was like to gather the bread from Heaven called "manna" in the book of Exodus (Exodus 16). What God did there is astonishing! The Lord fed His people, nearly two million of them, in the desert for forty years with bread that He caused to rain down from Heaven. Wherever they were, this bread was waiting for them each morning when they woke up. The instructions were specific but simple. They were to get up and gather it each morning before the heat of the day burns it away and not to try to store any for the next day. They were to gather and eat what they gathered that day. It is a picture of prayer. Just as the children of Israel had to get up and gather what they needed each day for that day, in the same way, you and I must go to the Lord each day to receive what we need for our day. This is why Jesus uses the words, ***"Give us this day our daily bread."***

3. Why is starting the day in prayer important?

_____

_____

_____

This reveals the second aspect of what prayer really is. Prayer is a relationship. Think about it. God, who is limitless in His power, ability, and resources, also has the desire to do certain things. The Bible says that nothing is too hard for the Lord (Genesis 18:14; Jeremiah 32:17, 27). In terms of power and ability, nothing can stop Him from doing what He wants to do. He has the ability to do whatever He desires. However, as we have mentioned before, He has chosen to limit Himself to our asking. In simple terms, there are things God wants to do, and has the ability to do, but does not do because we have not asked Him to do them. Again, James 4:2 (NKJV) says, ***"Yet you do not have because you do not ask."*** So we might ask, "Why? Why does God not just do those things? Why does He wait for me to ask?" The answer is that He wants a relationship. He wants us to join Him in what He is doing. It is like when my young daughter "helps" me build something. I do not need her help. I want it. If I am being honest, it is usually not all that helpful, always takes longer, and mistakes are made, but I do not care. It is because what I really want is time together. It is the giving of time, focus, and instruction of a dad to his daughter. It is a relationship. The same is true in prayer. God can do all He wants to do on His own. However, there are times He limits what He does to our asking. He wants us to be like children, seeing our needs, asking our Dad for His help, and joining with Him in what He does. All of that to say, this is why He tells us to come to Him today for our daily needs.

4. What is involved in a healthy relationship?

_____

_____

_____

In verse 12, we move from the outward to the inward. It goes from our physical needs to our spiritual needs. It is from the needs of the body to the needs of the heart. The focus of verse 12 is sin and its effects on us as people. Here it is called ***"debts." "Debts"*** comes from the Greek word "opheilema" and means "what is owed, what is due."

It refers to the way that sin piles up. Each offense is recorded and accounted for. Nothing is excused or overlooked and payment is required for each violation. This is just one of the staggering results of Jesus' sacrifice for our sins. He paid in full the price for every sin we have ever committed! Praise His blessed name.

Now, sin can be simply defined as anything God would not want us to do. Its effects are tragic on both the one sinning as well as those around them. Sin ravages lives. It takes and takes and takes and gives nothing in return. It has been said, "Sin will take you further than you want to go, cost you more than you want to pay, and keep you longer than you want to stay." It is true. Perhaps the most devious and destructive aspect of sin is its ability to separate us from what is good and right. Sin causes separation from all that is good. Especially damaging is its ability to cause relational separation. It separates husbands and wives, parents and kids, and people and God. As Christian people, we do not become unsaved by sin. Sin cannot take our salvation from us, but it does cause relational separation! Sin affects us deeply, it corrupts us and changes us. It makes us stupid! It causes us to distrust God, to turn from Him, and to distance ourselves from Him. Under sin's delusions and influence, we do not want God. We become self-sufficient and imagine that we **"have need of nothing"** (Revelation 3:17, NKJV). Nothing could be further from the truth.

5.   How does sin separate believers from the Lord?

_____

_____

_____

As sinful people, our great need is cleansing. We need the sin to be removed, washed away, forgiven, and forgotten. This forgiveness is needed not just from those we have sinned against, but ultimately from God. The reason for this is that all sin is first and foremost against God. We have broken His commands. Even if those we have sinned against forgive us, we have still sinned against God. So, true forgiveness can only come from God. Mark 2:7 (NKJV) says, *"Who can forgive sins but God alone?"* It is this that Jesus tells us to ask for.

6. Is there some sin you need to confess to God right now?

_____

_____

_____

Here we are told that we can simply ask God to *"forgive"* us. Consider that for a moment. In a world where people try continually and cannot absolve themselves, cleanse themselves, or fix their guilty consciences, we are told to simply come and ask. Our Lord could have said, "Work hard to have your good outweigh your bad and for every one thing you have done wrong you must atone in these three ways." He did not. He said to come and ask for forgiveness to be given and it will be. This is amazing grace! The word *"forgive"* here is one of my favorite words in the Greek language.

"Forgive" comes from the Greek verb "aphiemi" and means "to send away, to let go, dismiss." It is a reference to the way that sin was dealt with in the Old Testament sacrificial system of the Temple. Prior to the coming of the Lord Jesus Christ, sin was dealt with by animal sacrifice. The guilty man or woman would select an animal (a lamb) to be sacrificed on the altar as payment for their sin. The animal would be treated as the guilty one and die for the sins of the guilty man or woman. The innocent animal took the place of the guilty. It was a substitute. As the animal is offered and slaughtered, sin has been dealt with and the (formerly) guilty man or woman is now free to go. This freedom is our word *"forgive"* here. It means that nothing more is required. Sin has been dealt with and paid for. The sentence has been served. The guilty party is now dismissed.

7. How inconvenient would animal sacrifices be? How should that challenge us today?

_____

_____

_____

Notice the order of verse 12. It is first *"**forgive** us"* and then *"we **forgive**."* The order is critical as it is only once we have been forgiven that we will have the ability to forgive. The Bible regularly teaches us to forgive those who have sinned against us. However, it tells us to do so because we have been forgiven. Ephesians 4:32 (NKJV) says, ***"And be kind to one another, tenderhearted, forgiving one another, even as God in Christ forgave you."*** Forgiven people know what it is to be released from ***"debt."*** Therefore, they are able to release others. Here, our Lord tells us to ask Him to help us ***"forgive"*** others. Forgiveness is always a choice. It is always something we must choose to do. Many people put their offenders through a series of tests before they decide to extend forgiveness of any kind. Once the person has passed enough tests, forgiveness is given. This is not good! We are told by our Lord to make the decision to forgive right away because we have been forgiven. The prayer here is "I have decided to forgive because I have been forgiven. Lord, help me to actually do so."

8.   Have you felt God's forgiveness? If so, when? If not, why?

_____

_____

_____

9.   Is there someone you need to forgive?

_____

_____

_____

As we come into verse 13, we are still dealing with sin, but this time the prayer is for protection. The words ***"do not lead us into temptation"*** are really a prayer to be led away from temptation. ***"Lead"*** comes from the Greek verb "eisphero" and means "to bring along."

It describes someone who is following someone else. The prayer here is asking the Lord to point out the pitfalls, the holes, and the dangers along the way. It is a prayer for God to lead us away from what could cause us harm. This is not to say that if we do not pray for this, the Lord will lead us into sin. It is not, "Lord, if I do not ask you, you will lead me into temptation." No! Never. The Lord does not tempt us to sin. He cannot! James 1:13 (NKJV) makes this clear, **"Let no one say when he is tempted, 'I am tempted by God;' for God cannot be tempted by evil, nor does He Himself tempt anyone."** The prayer is one of dependency upon God to lead us away from what would entangle us. Hebrews 12:1 (NKJV) says that sin **"easily ensnares [traps]"** us. This is a prayer of protection. It is a prayer of humility that says, "I do not see and I do not know, but You do."

Not only is this part of the prayer a cry for protection from sin and temptation, but the words **"_deliver_ us from the evil one"** is asking for protection from an unseen enemy. **"_Deliver_"** comes from the Greek verb "rhoumai" which means to "rescue by snatching away, pulling to oneself."

This is what a parent would do with a child in the street when grabbing them quickly and pulling them to themselves out of danger. There is desperation in this request. This prayer comes from people who have taken seriously the words of the Lord Jesus who said about Satan, **"The thief does not come except to steal, and to kill, and to destroy"** (John 10:10, NKJV). Peter adds that the devil **"walks about like a roaring lion, seeking whom he may devour"** (1 Peter 5:8, NKJV). He is described as **"the evil one."** **"_Evil_"** comes from the Greek word "poneros" which means "worthless, wicked, vicious, malignant (infecting others)."

This word accurately describes our unseen enemy. How do you protect yourself from an invisible enemy that continually hunts you? He is an enemy that moves in the dark and changes shapes to deceive. It is an enemy who only wants to take every good thing from you, destroy your life, and ultimately kill you and your family. How do you stop an enemy like that? The answer is a prayer to the

One who sees all, who knows all, and who has all authority and power to protect us from the one who prowls in the dark. We run to Him who is greater to protect us from him who is less.

Lest we get swallowed up in the fear of sin or our unseen enemy, we are reminded of Who is really in charge. The end of verse 13 makes it clear that Jesus Christ is the King of kings and Lord of lords. He is infinitely stronger than the devil, any other angel, or ruler of men. We are to remind ourselves of this as we pray, *"For Yours is the kingdom and the power and the glory forever."* He is God. He is King. He is in charge. He is in control. This is a good thing to pause now and remind ourselves. There is only one real *"Kingdom"* and He is the King upon that throne. There is only one potentate and it is our Lord, Savior, King, and God. Satan will be judged and removed. Every wicked ruler of men will be judged and removed. He alone will rule and reign forever and ever. I cannot wait.

Our prayer should be, "We ask You for all that we need because you want to supply. We ask you to forgive us and to help us forgive others. We ask you, who is the One True King for your protection from our own sinful desires and our unseen enemy."

NOTES

LOVING NEIGHBORS

DEVOTION #1 - PASTOR JOHN CARTER

We are looking at prayer in a very in-depth way. We saw how Jesus taught us to approach God. Last week, we focused on how we are to, first and foremost, love God. This commandment is given to us throughout all of Scripture, both the Old and New Testaments. It is not a new concept. It has been around from the very beginning. Another not-so-new concept is the idea of loving others as ourselves. This is also known as the second greatest commandment and has been taught throughout Scripture from the very beginning.

Leviticus 19:18 says, *"You shall not take vengeance or bear a grudge against the sons of your own people, but you shall love your neighbor as yourself: I am the Lord."*

James 2:8 repeats the concept, *"If you really fulfill the royal law according to the Scripture, 'You shall love your neighbor as yourself,' you are doing well."*

Those are just a few of the examples that teach us this idea of loving our neighbor as ourselves. There are many more, and in fact, Matthew seems to carry quite a few repetitions of this passage in Leviticus. As we continue to break down the example of prayer that Jesus lays out for us in Matthew chapter 6, we will see Jesus using this aspect of the greatest commandments as the main theme of the prayer. Last week, we looked at the importance of loving the Lord with all our heart, soul, and mind through our prayer. This week, we are going to examine the idea of loving our neighbor as ourselves through our prayer life.

Matthew 6:11-13 says, *"Give us this day our daily bread, and forgive us our debts, as we also have forgiven our debtors. And lead us not into temptation, but deliver us from evil."* As we walk through each line of this model prayer, we will hopefully see the application of loving our neighbor through our prayer.

Let us start by first examining who exactly is our neighbor. When we hear the term "neighbor" we often only associate it with people who live right next door to our home. Interestingly enough, in Leviticus chapter 19, the idea of neighbor is clearly defined for us.

Leviticus 19:9-10 talks about not removing all of the harvests but leaving some *"for the poor and for the sojourner."* This is saying that your neighbor may not be in the same social economic status as you are, and it also implies that your neighbor may be just traveling through. It is not simply limited to the person that lives next door.

Verses 11-14 teach that we are not to lie and steal from one another. We are not to withhold wages that are due to those who earned them, nor are we to intentionally harm the deaf and the blind. This is showing us that our neighbor is the person with whom we work or hire. Our neighbor may have physical disabilities which we are to be compassionate towards.

Continuing through Leviticus chapter 19, verses 15-16 walk us through how we are to conduct ourselves within the structure of government and the court system. We are not to show partiality towards the powerful versus the poor. It is teaching us that our neighbor might be more than someone we live next to but also might be someone we find ourselves in court against.

Finally, in verses 17-18 of Leviticus 19, we see the connection of family brought right into the conversation of neighbor. It teaches us to not have hate in our hearts for our brothers (family); it directly ties that into neighbors. Verse 18 says, *"You shall not take vengeance or bear a grudge against the sons of your own people, but you shall love your neighbor as yourself: I am the Lord."* The implication is that your neighbor can also be your family.

Considering all the ways that another person can be your neighbor might seem overwhelming. In fact, our selfish nature is probably already saying, "What about me?" A good friend of mine was teaching me sales tactics and he said that when you are selling a product to a person, you always have to tune the radio to WII FM. That radio station (actually an acronym) is really the core question of our flesh, "What's In It For Me?" As a sales tactic, I get it, but we need to take this over to a spiritual application; "Does our prayer life resemble the radio station?" Do we only pray about the things that matter to us or benefit us? Please, do not misunderstand me when I say this. I am not saying God does not want to hear your heart. The question is meant to prompt you to consider others before you consider yourself. We are to be praying through the second greatest commandment of the Bible, loving your neighbor as yourself. Do we include in our prayers other peoples' petitions, requests, concerns, hurt, pain, or struggles with sin?

As we walk through what Jesus lays out in this prayer, I hope and pray you will see Him point us back to the fundamental aspects of the Christian walk. We are to be loving God and loving others, especially through our prayer life.

DAILY PROVISION COMES FROM THE FATHER
DEVOTION #2 - PASTOR JOHN CARTER

"Give us this day our daily bread." Matthew 6:11

This verse should be put in context with the previous week where we realize and understand that God knows our needs. Jesus shows that after we give God all this praise, honor, and glory, He comes back to a basic need we have (only with a twist). It is *"our daily bread."* Food is such an important element of our physical survival. Jesus, in previous verses, taught us that our Heavenly Father knows what we are in need of. Here, He is pointing to something that is not physical but rather spiritual. We need to put some more Scripture to this so we can put it in full context.

Jesus, in previous chapters, points to this very aspect of our need for spiritual food or nourishment. Matthew 4:4 says, *"But he answered, 'It is written, 'Man shall not live by bread alone, but by every word that comes from the mouth of God.'"* Matthew 5:6 adds, *"Blessed are those who hunger and thirst for righteousness, for they shall be satisfied."*

These are the verses from the previous chapter before Jesus teaches us the model prayer. These are Jesus' very words. It includes every word, and also a *"hunger and thirst for righteousness."* We need to understand that our need for spiritual food and spiritual nourishment has to be at the forefront of our prayer life. When was the last time you asked God to show you something in His Word that you did not understand? Have you studied His Word to gain understanding and truth? Like we are doing with this passage in Matthew chapter 6, have you ever dug deep into the meaning and intent of the passage? Do you see this "digging" as the instruction from God to desire spiritual food? Do you hunger after the things that are right and true? Are you learning to live your life by *"every word"*? Do not just accept the words you like and desire to be true, but literally every word!

That is a hard one to swallow. It is easier for us not to self-examine our spiritual state and hunger than it is to say, "Nope, I need to change my priorities." Saying them is one thing, but acting on them is totally different. Just to make sure the full context of what Jesus is teaching here is clear, later in Matthew 6:33, Jesus says, *"But seek first the kingdom of God and his righteousness, and all these things will be added to you."*

Jesus is not inconsistent with His teaching. In fact, this has been the teaching from the beginning of the Bible. Learn God's ways and live them out. Learn what God considers righteous and walk in them. Seek and hunger after His commandments and make sure you are walking in them.

It is very important that I put this caveat in here. I am not speaking of walking in God's ways in a salvific manner. That is to say, salvation does not come by solely walking in God's ways or walking in His righteousness. John 6:35 says, *"Jesus said to them, 'I am the bread of life; whoever comes to me shall not hunger, and whoever believes in me shall never thirst.'"*

In the book of John, Jesus is recorded as teaching that He is the very source of life and He is the ultimate source of salvation. When He teaches us to seek first the Kingdom of God and its righteousness in Matthew, He is saying that you had better know Him first. Without Jesus, we have nothing. Paul points to our lives without Christ as being filthy rags. When we talk of walking in the way and example of Christ, it is after we know Him. That is where we see Jesus directing us in this model prayer. We need daily spiritual food and daily living water. We need to be daily rooted in God's Word to know and understand what God desires from us.

I love that in this model prayer Jesus uses plural words. He says, *"Give us."* He did not say, "give them," or "give me." I believe this is intentional. We need each other to grow. We need one another to build up and to encourage, but also to keep us from falling into our own foolish, fleshly way of thinking. We need each other to say, "Hey, I was reading this passage and this makes no sense to me at all. Can you help me through it?" It might be, "I was reading this passage, and WOW; God showed me what it means and how to apply it to my life!" This aspect of growing (becoming more like Christ) is not a journey you take all on your own. This is why God gave us neighbors. This is why God gave us each other! If you are not sure who your neighbor is read yesterday's devotion. Consider today a person (neighbor) that you can encourage. It might be helpful just to tell them you are praying for them. It could be helpful to share a passage of Scripture that has meant a lot to you. Act in a manner that God tells you to respond. Maybe it means inviting them out for coffee or lunch and just sharing all the amazing things God is teaching you. Do something in this regard of being fed daily with the spiritual food that God gives and share it with your neighbor.

1 Corinthians 10:1-6 says, *"For I do not want you to be unaware, brothers, that our fathers were all under the cloud, and all passed through the sea, and all were baptized into Moses in the cloud and in the sea, and all ate the same spiritual food, and all drank the same spiritual drink. For they drank from the spiritual Rock that followed them, and the Rock was Christ. Nevertheless, with most of them God was not pleased, for they were overthrown in the wilderness. Now these things took place as examples for us, that we might not desire evil as they did."*

Today, we recognize our holy Father's Kingdom. It is where our nourishment comes from. We need to pursue goodness and His righteousness. Pursue it together with your neighbors!

FORGIVENESS EXAMPLED AND ILLUSTRATED
DEVOTION #3 - PASTOR JOHN CARTER

"And forgive us our debts, as we also have forgiven our debtors." Matthew 6:12

Why is it so hard for us to forgive others? If you have been a part of the church for any amount of time, you have, more than likely, heard a message about forgiveness. We love to hear about how we are forgiven and we love to receive the forgiveness of others when we wrong them, but it seems too hard to give it out ourselves. That always seems to be the hardest thing to do! We are going to dive deeper into forgiveness next week. In fact, we are going to dedicate the entire week's devotions to it. So, today, as we examine what Jesus is saying and teaching us in prayer, we cannot exclude this aspect of forgiveness.

Forgiveness has two parts. There is repentance and then there is forgiveness. Jesus, in this model prayer, is asking us to focus on both of these aspects. Repentance is the acknowledgment of wrong and then turning away. It can include the reconciliation or forgiveness of that wrong. Not only is Jesus pointing to these two concepts of forgiveness, but He is also teaching us the duality of this role that we have in each of us. We each need to go before the Lord and recognize the areas we have wronged God the Father, and not only recognize it, but repent of it. This is what God does when He forgives us. He expects us to be genuinely sorrowful and to desire to never turn to sin again. It is true repentance.

In 1 John 2:1-3, we read, *"My little children, I am writing these things to you so that you may not sin. But if anyone does sin, we have an advocate with the Father, Jesus Christ the righteous. He is the propitiation for our sins, and not for ours only but also for the sins of the whole world. And by this we know that we have come to know him, if we keep his commandments."*

I love this passage. I think it shows the awesome love of Jesus and the Father for us. The call is first that we, who are the children of God, do not sin. However, our fleshly nature is known to take its toll. When we do sin, we have an advocate, someone to step in on our behalf. I love that! This passage ultimately points to the position our heart takes towards the instruction and commandments of God. It is that we will desire to keep them. It is not that we actually keep them perfectly all the time, but that our hearts' desire is that we will strive to keep them. Just like Jesus teaches us in the model prayer, when we screw up, we are quick to repent and ask for forgiveness. Jesus is simply teaching that we ought not to approach God without thinking about the offensive ways and sins we have caused to a holy, righteous God. We must recognize that those sins were washed with the blood of His Son, Jesus.

Jesus is also correlating this forgiveness we have received from God to something that we do for one another. We love to receive it and claim it for our own sins, but it is all so challenging when we are asked to give some of that forgiveness, or mercy, to others. Even when it is hard, God still asks us to do it! Therefore, it is not impossible! It is just uncomfortable, or not in our nature. I think this is also why Jesus was sure to put this in His example of prayer. He knew we would need to be reminded over and over again of the fact that we have received His awesome forgiveness, so we need to share that with our neighbor. There are many passages of Scripture that deal with this teaching. The Bible, from the Old Testament to the New Testament, teaches forgiveness, mercy, and grace. Listen to David's heart of repentance. This really sets the tone for how our hearts ought to sound when we approach God regarding our sins.

In Psalm 51:1-19, David says, *"Have mercy on me, O God, according to your steadfast love; according to your abundant mercy blot out my transgressions. Wash me thoroughly from my iniquity, and cleanse me from my sin! For I know my transgressions, and my sin is ever before me. Against you, you only, have I sinned and done what is evil in your sight, so that you may be justified in your words and blameless in your judgment. Behold, I was brought forth in iniquity, and in sin did my mother conceive me. Behold, you delight in truth in the inward being, and you teach me wisdom in the secret heart. Purge me with hyssop, and I shall be clean; wash me, and I shall be whiter than snow. Let me hear joy and gladness; let the bones that you have broken rejoice. Hide your face from my sins, and blot out all my iniquities. Create in me a clean heart, O God, and renew a right spirit within me. Cast me not away from your presence, and take not your Holy Spirit from me. Restore to me the joy of your salvation, and uphold me with a willing spirit. Then I will teach transgressors your ways, and sinners will return to you. Deliver me from bloodguiltiness, O God, O God of my salvation, and my tongue will sing aloud of your righteousness. O Lord, open my lips, and my mouth will declare your praise. For you will not delight in sacrifice, or I would give it; you will not be pleased with a burnt offering. The sacrifices of God are a broken spirit; a broken and contrite heart, O God, you will not despise. Do good to Zion in your good pleasure; build up the walls of Jerusalem; then will you delight in right sacrifices, in burnt offerings and whole burnt offerings; then bulls will be offered on your altar."*

Do we respond this way to God about our sins? Do we approach Him with this kind of repentant heart? Do we respond the way God does toward our sins? Do we hold a grudge against our neighbor for the harm, hurt, or damage they have caused us? Take time today to reflect on forgiveness, both the forgiveness you receive as well as the forgiveness you ought to give to your neighbor.

DO NOT LEAD US INTO TEMPTATION

DEVOTION #4 - PASTOR JOHN CARTER

"And lead us not into temptation." Matthew 6:13

Jesus is bringing to the very forefront of prayer these elements of our life that need to be addressed. He points us to the spiritual food we need, the righteousness of God, and the amazing forgiving love of our Father. Now, He walks us through how to overcome the fleshly temptations of the world. This is ultimately the walk of a confessing believer, a Christian. It is learning to walk in the ways of righteousness, mimicking the behavior of Jesus, walking in mercy and grace, and learning to resist the devil and his temptations.

Listen to some of the apostles' and early church leaders' teachings on this idea of temptation.

In 1 Corinthians 10:12-13, Paul says, *"Therefore let anyone who thinks that he stands take heed lest he fall. No temptation has overtaken you that is not common to man. God is faithful, and he will not let you be tempted beyond your ability, but with the temptation he will also provide the way of escape, that you may be able to endure it."*

In James 1:13-15, James writes, *"Let no one say when he is tempted, 'I am being tempted by God,' for God cannot be tempted with evil, and he himself tempts no one. But each person is tempted when he is lured and enticed by his own desire. Then desire when it has conceived gives birth to sin, and sin when it is fully grown brings forth death."*

Jesus is saying we ought to ask God to keep us from temptation. Another way to say it might be to ask God to give you the ability to resist the devil, the evil one. We see that God Himself is not the tempter. He does not tempt anyone with evil, nor does He tempt anyone. However, the devil, the one like a lion seeking whom he can devour, is very much given the name of tempter, or accuser. In fact, in Matthew chapter 4, we learn of Jesus' teaching on bread and spiritual food we see a special name given, *"And the tempter came and said to him, 'If you are the Son of God, command these stones to become loaves of bread'"* (Matthew 4:3).

The tempter is the one who tries to get Jesus to relinquish His heavenly authority and submit to the authority of the flesh. The tempter uses the very substance of food as a tool to tempt Jesus. We know the tempter uses way more than just food to get us to submit to our flesh.

What are your temptations? Do you know what they are? Do you ask God to give you strength over them? Do you ask God to keep the tempter away from you? Have you set up safeguards against your temptations? What is your method for overcoming them? In Jesus' teaching us how to pray, He is sure to teach us that the way to victory is indeed through prayer. Often times, we may view prayer as the last effective method to overcome our temptation; however, in Matthew chapter 6, Jesus is teaching us that prayer is essential to overcoming the temptations of the devil.

In 2 Corinthians 10:3-6, Paul says, *"For though we walk in the flesh, we are not waging war according to the flesh. For the weapons of our warfare are not of the flesh but have divine power to destroy strongholds. We destroy arguments and every lofty opinion raised against the knowledge of God, and take every thought captive to obey Christ, being ready to punish every disobedience, when your obedience is complete."*

Paul is saying that we have to be of the mind that is ready and willing to obey versus the mind that is ready and willing to disobey. He says it like this to the church of Rome in Romans 6:12-14, *"Let not sin therefore reign in your mortal body, to make you obey its passions. Do not present your members [body] to sin as instruments for unrighteousness, but present yourselves to*

God as those who have been brought from death to life, and your members to God as instruments for righteousness. For sin will have no dominion over you, since you are not under law [the law of sin and death] but under grace."

Romans 6:17-18 adds, *"But thanks be to God, that you who were once slaves of sin have become obedient from the heart to the standard of teaching to which you were committed, and, having been set free from sin, have become slaves of righteousness."*

Romans 8:5-8 says, *"For those who live according to the flesh set their minds on the things of the flesh, but those who live according to the Spirit set their minds on the things of the Spirit. For to set the mind on the flesh is death, but to set the mind on the Spirit is life and peace. For the mind that is set on the flesh is hostile to God, for it does not submit to God's law; indeed, it cannot. Those who are in the flesh cannot please God."*

Romans 8:11 states, *"If the Spirit of him who raised Jesus from the dead dwells in you, he who raised Christ Jesus from the dead will also give life to your mortal bodies through his Spirit who dwells in you."*

I know there is a lot in those passages of Romans. I would love to spend hours walking through them. I gave you a few passages to help illustrate the point of Matthew chapter 6, and hopefully, give you some powerful words of encouragement through Paul's writings. Paul is talking about obedience and freedom and how we now, as believers who have the Holy Spirit, are to live out our life. That is talking about the present, current state of your body. Our body is mortal now, but will be immortal when we are made in the likeness of Jesus. I love these passages in Romans. There are many more that I like, but these bring me incredible encouragement. The first thing we see in Romans 6:12-14 is that Paul instructs us to not let sin *"reign"* in our mortal body. This means that sin is something that can be conquered and is something that believers can have victory over. It is something we experience in our *"mortal body."*

He continues with where and how this change can occur. It starts with a change of heart, a submission to sound teaching. He says that freedom from sin comes when we are willing to submit and walk in righteousness. Paul has a flare for the dramatic and says to be a slave to righteousness. In other words, obey it at all costs.

In Romans chapter 8, Paul continues to take us through this aspect of walking in the flesh and giving into temptation versus walking in the way of God and becoming a slave to righteousness. The contrast between where we allow our minds to dwell is really what Paul is focusing on. In Romans 8:11, Paul gives us his major point and that is the power of the Holy Spirit dwells in us. I do not know if you caught this or not, but I want it to be noted. The word *"mortal body"* shows up again in verse 11. Paul says that the Spirit who raised Jesus from the dead, God's Holy Spirit, is the same Spirit that we can depend on in these *"mortal bodies"* to overcome and have victory over sin! I tell you, when I wrapped my head around this teaching of Paul, it helped me so much. I did not have to give into sin every time even though my body is made of flesh and desires fleshly things. I have the Spirit that is dwelling in me. That is far more powerful than my own flesh. I have the Holy Spirit who will help me overcome my fleshly temptations. If you are a believer, you have that same Holy Spirit in you. You can overcome your temptation and you do not have to give in to sin.

Praise God today and ask Him to give you the strength to overcome the temptations that reside in your life. Lean on the power of the Holy Spirit to help you overcome temptation. Be willing to walk hand in hand to help your brother and sister in Christ to overcome those temptations.

DELIVER US FROM THE EVIL ONE
DEVOTION #5 - PASTOR JOHN CARTER

"And lead us not into temptation, but deliver us from evil."
Matthew 6:13

As we have been walking through this section of the Sermon on the Mount, we see Jesus pointing us to deliverance. If we are going to be delivered, we have to identify from what we need to be delivered. It is like when we talk about being saved in the church, if you do not clearly identify what it is you need saving from, salvation sounds really weird. Jesus does not make it a profound mystery. He says it right here in the example, *"Deliver us from evil."* I want to give you a couple of correlating passages that follow along with the concept of evil. Some of your translations may even have this evil identified as the evil one.

Read these verses and see if you can connect some dots:

- *"I have given them your word, and the world has hated them because they are not of the world, just as I am not of the world. I do not ask that you take them out of the world, but that you keep them from the evil one. They are not of the world, just as I am not of the world. Sanctify them in the truth; your word is truth."* John 17:14-17

- *"Finally, brothers, pray for us, that the word of the Lord may speed ahead and be honored, as happened among you, and that we may be delivered from wicked and evil men. For not all have faith. But the Lord is faithful. He will establish you and guard you against the evil one."* 2 Thessalonians 3:1-3

- *"But the Lord stood by me and strengthened me, so that through me the message might be fully proclaimed and all the Gentiles might hear it. So I was rescued from the lion's mouth. The Lord will rescue me from every evil deed and bring me safely into his heavenly kingdom. To him be the glory forever and ever. Amen."* 2 Timothy 4:17-18

Some translations and manuscripts include some words at the end of the Lord's Prayer. Right after *"deliver us from evil,"* they may include these words, *"For Yours is the kingdom and the power and the glory, forever. Amen"* (Matthew 6:13, NKJV).

Whether it is included or not is really not a major point. The idea that God's Kingdom has the power and glory to overcome evil or the evil one is clearly articulated in the verses prior and throughout Scripture. It is always important to consider this when we are praying. Are we cognizant of the evil that is in our world? Do we seek the One who has power over the evil one to protect us? Consider some of the following verses:

- *"And you were dead in the trespasses and sins in which you once walked, following the course of this world, following the prince of the power of the air, the spirit that is now at work in the sons of disobedience - among whom we all once lived in the passions of our flesh, carrying out the desires of the body and the mind, and were by nature children of wrath, like the rest of mankind."* Ephesians 2:1-3

- *"Finally, be strong in the Lord and in the strength of his might. Put on the whole armor of God, that you may be able to stand against the schemes of the devil. For we do not wrestle against flesh and blood, but against the rulers, against the authorities, against the cosmic powers over this present darkness, against the spiritual forces of evil in the heavenly places."* Ephesians 6:10-12

- *"We know that everyone who has been born of God does not keep on sinning, but he who was born of God protects him, and the evil one does not touch him. We know that we are from God, and the whole world lies in the power of the evil one."* 1 John 5:18-19

- *"Be sober-minded; be watchful. Your adversary the devil prowls around like a roaring lion, seeking someone to devour. Resist him, firm in your faith, knowing that the same kinds of suffering are being experienced by your brotherhood throughout the world."* 1 Peter 5:8-9

As I read through those texts (there are many more I could have included), the thing that sticks out is that an evil power definitely exists in our world. The desire of the evil one is to destroy, consume, create chaos, and ruin our lives. The markers of those who are walking in the kingdom of darkness are disobedience, wrath, and living out of the desires and passions of the flesh. The devil (evil one) has schemes, traps, tricks, or temptations that he sets out to trip us up. Jesus, when He modeled this prayer for us, wants us to be aware of these traps and recognize there is evil that we need to be aware of. He points us to seek that help from the Father. He is the One who is all-powerful and mighty! Consider the evil that may be surrounding you today. Go to the Father and ask for Him to deliver you from this evil. He has the power to do that! Scripture also teaches us that this battle against the evil one is not one that is fought on our own. Obviously, we need the presence and power of God, but God also gave us each other (our neighbors if you will), to help overcome the temptations of the evil one. Below are a few passages that really show the the need we have for one another and overcoming the traps and temptation of the evil one:

- *"If we say we have fellowship with him while we walk in darkness, we lie and do not practice the truth. But if we walk in the light, as he is in the light, we have fellowship with one another, and the blood of Jesus his Son cleanses us from all sin."* 1 John 1:6-7

- *"Brothers, if anyone is caught in any transgression, you who are spiritual should restore him in a spirit of gentleness. Keep watch on yourself, lest you too be tempted. Bear one another's burdens, and so fulfill the law of Christ."* Galatians 6:1-2

- *"Therefore, confess your sins to one another and pray for one another, that you may be healed. The prayer of a righteous person has great power as it is working."* James 5:16

Today, as you are praying, lift up your brother or sister in Christ. Carry some of their burdens as you approach God and pray on their behalf. Pray that the Lord will deliver you both from evil.

LOVING YOUR NEIGHBOR

DEVOTION #6 - PASTOR JOHN CARTER

Today, we are going to reflect on this week's main passage. Jesus is teaching us some really important things about the power of prayer. Matthew 6:11-13 says, *"Give us this day our daily bread, and forgive us our debts, as we also have forgiven our debtors. And lead us not into temptation, but deliver us from evil."*

If you missed one of the deeper explanations of these verses, let me encourage you to go back and walk through them. I pray you will find them challenging and encouraging. In every aspect of this week's study of the Lord's Prayer, there is an element of how showing love to our neighbor, and ultimately to our fellow brothers and sisters in Christ, plays an important role in our prayer life.

Community is so important for the believer's walk and growth in Christ. Let me ask you a question, "Do you have a serious commitment to walk with a community of believers?" We live in a world that can be more connected to each other than at any time in history, yet community seems to be one of the greatest longings people have. I think I need to clarify this a little. When I say community, I am not talking about a facade of people that share some small things in common like sports, work, or hobbies. When I talk about community, I am talking about people that you can be real with. It is people you can be authentic with. I know that idea of authenticity is scary. What if they do not like the real you? What if they are not anything like you? I would rather be real and genuine with someone than have to put on a facade or a fake front. The church body is made up of many different kinds of people; that is a fact. Some of those people think through things in a completely different manner. Guess what? We need "different" in our life. We need people that are not exactly like us so that we can learn to better each other. This idea of community is not just some random idea I have, it is actually in the Bible:

- *"For as in one body we have many members, and the members do not all have the same function, so we, though many, are one body in Christ, and individually members one of another."* Romans 12:4-5

- *"For just as the body is one and has many members, and all the members of the body, though many, are one body, so it is with Christ. For in one Spirit we were all baptized into one body - Jews or Greeks, slaves or free - and all were made to drink of one Spirit. For the body does not consist of one member but of many."* 1 Corinthians 12:12-14

- *"Therefore, having put away falsehood, let each one of you speak the truth with his neighbor, for we are members one of another."* Ephesians 4:25

Being in community with one another is all throughout Scripture. I just listed some of the major ones, but there are so many that teach about this idea of being there for one another. The Old Testament teaches it in the form of loving your neighbor. Jesus also teaches it in this context of loving your neighbor. Today, as you are preparing to gather together with one another tomorrow, consider how you can get connected with the community. Maybe it means making yourself vulnerable. Are you willing to put it out there that you need and desire a community to be real and authentic with? If you do not want to wait until Sunday, just text "riverconnect" to 97000 and ask if there is a community of believers that is meeting near you. We call them Growth Communities. Who knows, they might be getting together tonight. You could find yourself connecting with a group of fellow believers that love God and are learning how to love one another.

Let me leave you with this passage in Hebrews. Consider how you can do this today for someone you know. Hebrews 10:24-25 says, *"And let us consider how to stir up one another to love and good works, not neglecting to meet together, as is the habit of some, but encouraging one another, and all the more as you see the Day drawing near."*

You can do this by getting to know someone more than just the surface stuff. It means to really be genuine in getting to know them. Get to know them so well you can authentically pray for them. You can pray against the temptations the evil one will set before them. That is really getting to know someone. Maybe you need to open up, and know you are not alone. God gave us each other so we could have help when we face adversity, temptation, and trials. Share it with someone. Let them encourage you. Be blessed and look forward to gathering together tomorrow as the church.

LESSON SIX

Forgiveness

PASTOR CHUCK LINDSEY

"For if you forgive men their trespasses, your heavenly Father will also forgive you. But if you do not forgive men their trespasses, neither will your Father forgive your trespasses." Matthew 6:14-15 (NKJV)

1. What does the word *"trespasses"* mean? What are some common examples?

    _____

    _____

    _____

A question I am often asked as a pastor is, "Do I have to forgive someone who is not asking for forgiveness?" Behind that question is a desire for the person who has wronged us to see their error, feel sorry for it, and come to us for forgiveness. I have seen more unicorns in my life than I have ever had this happen! I am joking, of course. I have never had this happen. The question comes out of hurt and is asking whether we are justified to withhold forgiveness until the person recognizes their wrong. My answer to it is always the same, "Read Matthew 6:14. What does it say? Notice that there is no mention of the person asking us for forgiveness." Again, this is rare to ever have happened. Most people, even if they recognize the wrong, do not say anything about it and just move on.

2. Have you wronged someone (or they perceived it that way), asked for forgiveness, and did not receive forgiveness from them? How did it feel?

    _____

    _____

    _____

Jesus does not say, "When you are asked for forgiveness, go ahead and extend it." He says that we must actively choose to *"**forgive**."* *"**Forgive**"* comes from the Greek word "aphiemi" and means "to send away, dismiss, or release requirements."

The Greek text here makes it clear that this forgiveness is something we must decide to do regardless of what the other person does or does not do. The word *"**forgive**"* in the Greek text is in the aorist tense and active voice which simply means that it is something that we must actively decide to do. We choose to send away the wrong and require no more from the person who hurt us. Interestingly, the word *"**forgive**"* is also in the subjunctive mood in Greek and so it means that this is a question. In other words, it is what we should decide to do, but will we do it?

3. What are some advantages of forgiving others?

_____

_____

_____

Forgiveness is not easy to genuinely give. It often requires a choice to give it over and over. This is why in verse 14, Jesus gives us some motivation. The tone of verse 14 is, "This is why you should." He says, *"If you forgive men their trespasses, your heavenly Father will also forgive you."* Notice the conditions here. If we forgive others, He forgives us. However, in verse 15, we read, *"But, if you do not forgive men their trespasses, neither will your Father forgive your trespasses."* Wait, is this saying God will not forgive me if I do not forgive others? That is right. Let me explain. First, this is not referring to salvation. It is referring to fellowship or communion with God. It is referring to our daily repentance from sin in order to maintain a clear conscience. In 1 John 1:9, it says, *"If we confess our sins, He is faithful and just to forgive us our sins and to cleanse us from all unrighteousness."* This is not referring to salvation, but rather the regular cleansing from God that we need as sinful people. As true followers of Christ, we do not want to sin, but still do and will continue to until we go home or He returns. We will not become sinless this side of Heaven. However, as His people, we should sin less as the years go by and as we grow in Him. Repentance from daily sin is a key component in our growth. When we sin, we turn to our Lord with remorse and for His forgiveness and cleansing.

4. Summarize this last paragraph in your own words. What thoughts come to mind?

_____

_____

_____

The warning in verses 14-15 is against thinking we can withhold forgiveness from others and still be "good" with God. It is not so! It is a contradiction to ask God for His forgiveness for our sin against Him, to ask Him to release us from our wrongdoing, and at the same time refuse to give it to someone who has sinned against us. Jesus is teaching us an important biblical principle. He basically says, "If you refuse to release the wrongs of someone else, I will not release the wrongs you have committed against Me." This is a withholding of the sense that we are "clean" before the Lord, that sin has been dealt with, and that things are right between Him and me. He withholds this to force us to do what we are supposed to do. Believe it or not, this is God's mercy towards us. It is designed to make us do what is best for us to do.

5. How is God's discipline a gift to us?

_____

_____

_____

We all know that unforgiveness is destructive. It has been said, "Unforgiveness is like drinking poison and waiting for the other person to die." That is so true. All of this is designed by God to prevent something that I see often as a pastor. It is a familiar scene. The husband and wife walk into my office separately. They are visibly cold towards each other. They sit apart. They do not touch, make no eye contact, and do not speak towards each other at all. They begin to explain their marriage troubles. After some time, I begin to ask questions. The first question is always something along the lines of, "Tell me about your relationship with the Lord Jesus." Nearly every time, they seemed surprised by my question (as in, "What does this have to do with anything?") and then tell me that things are great with them and God. It is not true. It is never true. As Jesus says here, it cannot be true.

6. How does our relationship with God affect our fellowship with others?

_____

_____

_____

7. How does our relationship with others affect our fellowship with God?

_____

_____

_____

Peter warns in 1 Peter 3:7 (NKJV) that it is possible to have our prayers **"hindered"** (In Greek the word means to "cut off or cut short") if we deal with our spouses the wrong way. Psalm 66:18 (NKJV) says, **"If I regard iniquity in my heart, the Lord will not hear."**

8. How do these verses emphasize the importance of forgiveness?

_____

_____

_____

Our Lord said in Matthew 5:23-24 that if we begin to approach God and remember that there is something between us and another person, we are to leave our gift and go make it right with the other person. All of this teaches that we cannot create brokenness in our relationships with others, ignore it, and think that nothing is broken between us and God. In God's mercy, He has connected these things. It forces us to forgive others, to work towards reconciliation (if it is possible), and to make things right in order for us to be "right" with God.

9. How does pride relate to forgiveness?

_____

_____

_____

Jesus basically says, "Choose to send away the wrong that has been done to you, just as I have sent away the wrong you have done to Me. If you refuse to do so, I will make you aware that you and I are not right until you decide to."

NOTES

WALKING THROUGH FORGIVENESS
DEVOTION #1 - PASTOR JOHN CARTER

This week, we are going to look into Scripture regarding the aspect of forgiveness. We have been walking through Jesus' teachings on many different things that need to be applied to our life. We see forgiveness as a very important part of our Christian walk. Jesus has been teaching us how we are to practice our righteousness. It is a practice that is much different than most religious practices (Matthew 6:1). In contrast to being noticed by men, Jesus teaches that we need to realize and focus on the fact that God the Father sees us and knows what we are doing. Jesus has taught us how we are to practice giving to the needy and poor and in what manner we are to do this. Jesus has talked through the amazing privilege and power of prayer and how to practice it in the every day. In Matthew 6:14-15, Jesus continues to teach us some very real and practical things we are to practice in our walk and obedience to Him regarding forgiveness, *"For if you forgive others their trespasses, your heavenly Father will also forgive you, but if you do not forgive others their trespasses, neither will your Father forgive your trespasses."*

I think it is important to refresh our memory on the previous verse to give us a bit of context. In the Lord's Prayer, Jesus laid down a foundation for this very subject of forgiveness. Matthew 6:12-13 says, *"And forgive us our debts, as we also have forgiven our debtors. And lead us not into temptation, but deliver us from evil."*

We see Jesus connecting in verse 12 the aspect of forgiveness being linked to this application of debt. While we have expounded on these verses in the previous week, it is important to understand the context we are now walking through. The link between debt and trespasses as it correlates to forgiveness, is a teaching that has existed in Scripture from the beginning. Sin is often closely linked to the very practical understanding of debt. As we mature in this world, eventually you may have to take on debt, whether it is to purchase a car or buy a home. Debt, unfortunately, becomes something we tend to just live with and have as part of our everyday life. We adjust our finances and we make plans financially based a lot of times on how much debt we carry. Many of you may feel like you have your financial debt under control. We use keywords in our society like "managing debt" and "debt consolidation" to help us position ourselves where we want to be financially. Now imagine if we had absolutely no debt. That would mean no mortgage, no car payment, no credit card bills, no medical bills, and no other financial obligations. It was all eliminated and we were free from the financial burden that comes with having debt. What would you do? Would you run to the bank and take on more debt? I would certainly hope not. Would you be excited that the pressures from having loans had been released, or forgiven? Would you find yourself not doing a certain job because you do not have to pay the bills (loans)? Would you choose to spend more time with your spouse, or with your kids? Maybe you would plan some kind of vacation that you always wanted but never had the time or money because of the amount of debt you carried.

I love how God gives us things to relate to in this life that help us understand heavenly things. This aspect of debt and trespasses is a direct, relatable correlation to sin and iniquity towards God Himself. I find this link between debt and trespasses to be a very profound connection because it helps us understand God's behavior. God so desperately wants us to understand and know how it feels to be His children. He also wants us to understand how we are to emulate His behavior. He gives us these real and practical object lessons so we can better understand His heart of love, His motive, and ultimately His amazing instructions for our life.

So today, take time to take account (just like in the financial sense) of your debts. This may be thinking through something you have done against someone else; that is to say, debts you owe to other people. It may be that you have a record of someone wronging you;

that is to say, you know of other people that owe you. Maybe you have held onto this debt for a long time, maybe months, years, or even decades. No one ever wants to admit the fact that they are holding a grudge, but sometimes it is easier to hold a grudge than to actually walk through forgiveness. Is that you?

We know God desires authenticity. We have studied this in the past weeks. Do you have hurt and pain that you have held onto from your mom and dad? What about your siblings? Do you have pain and hurt that has been rooted in you since you were a little child? Maybe you have been hurt by a spouse, an "ex" that totally broke your trust. Have your kids hurt you? Maybe your kids keep taking advantage of you over and over again. As we start to examine all the ways in which we can be hurt or process pain, unfortunately, we soon find out there are many ways that we can be hurt. There are many people that can easily harm us or hurt us. This harm or hurt is rooted in the fact that there is also deep love. It is a love that was maybe betrayed. I know this hurt and pain very well in my own life. There have been seriously damaging pain and hurt that I personally have had to walk through. Let me tell you, it is not fun; however, it is completely necessary. You may need to take some time and ask God to help you walk through this pain. I do not think it was an accident that Jesus taught us how to pray before He walked us through how to forgive. Trust me when I say this, He (Jesus) knows your hurt better than anyone! He also knows how to heal your hurt better than anyone else!

After evaluating your records of debt that may be owed to you because of wrongs (trespasses) that have been committed against you, now do this. Take account of your trespasses (sins) against God. Do you know what they are? Do you even consider them to be debts against God? Maybe you have sins that have never been dealt with; in other words, they are long overdue. They may be sins that you have walked in for months, years, or maybe even decades.

If you are anything like me, when I compare the two lists, the debts against me compared to the debts I have against God, it is dramatically different. They honestly do not even compare. The debts that I have accumulated against God grossly outweigh any debt that I could collect against someone else.

As we conclude, maybe today you can spend some time walking through this very aspect of forgiveness in your own life. Have you received the forgiveness of God? Make sure this is something you have received! If you have questions or would like to know more about how to receive this forgiveness, text "riverconnect" to 97000 and we will be sure to reach out to you. If you have received the forgiveness of God in your life, how have you found this forgiveness applied to others?

REPENTANCE IS KEY

DEVOTION #2 - PASTOR JOHN CARTER

Yesterday, we started to develop the idea of forgiveness as it relates to debt. We walked through a short exercise comparing all that we have done against God versus what others may have done wrong against us. It reminded me of one of Jesus' parables that He taught. Please read the following passage. Spend some time meditating on how similar the teaching in the parable is compared to the passage in Matthew 6:14-15. Maybe there is something that Jesus is trying to teach us that we really need to understand.

Matthew 18:21-35 says, *"Then Peter came up and said to him, 'Lord, how often will my brother sin against me, and I forgive him? As many as seven times?' Jesus said to him, 'I do not say to you seven times, but seventy-seven times. Therefore the kingdom of heaven may be compared to a king who wished to settle accounts with his servants. When he began to settle, one was brought to him who owed him ten thousand talents. And since he could not pay, his master ordered him to be sold, with his wife and children and all that he had, and payment to be made. So the servant fell on his knees, imploring him, 'Have patience with me, and I will pay you everything.' And out of pity for him, the master of that servant released him and forgave him the debt. But when that same servant went out, he found one of his fellow servants who owed him a hundred denarii, and seizing him, he began to choke him, saying, 'Pay what you owe.' So his fellow servant fell down and pleaded with him, 'Have patience with me, and I will pay you.' He refused and went and put him in prison until he should pay the debt. When his fellow servants saw what had taken place, they were greatly distressed, and they went and reported to their master all that had taken place. Then his master summoned him and said to him, 'You wicked servant! I forgave you all that debt because you pleaded with me. And should not you have had mercy on your fellow servant, as I had mercy on you?' And in anger his master delivered him to the jailers, until he should pay all his debt. So also my heavenly Father will do to every one of you, if you do not forgive your brother from your heart.'"*

This is a very shocking parable that Jesus speaks to us. As believers and followers of Jesus Christ, we have been given a great amount of mercy and forgiveness from God. Do we live out this forgiveness we have received from God like the servant in the parable? Or, do we, as verse 35 teaches us, choose to forgive our brothers, sisters, moms, dads, or whomever it may be? Are you doing it from your heart? If we are 100% honest, that is probably the hardest part to do. As a father, I often have to instruct my children to say, "I am sorry," for some wrong they have done against their sibling. If you are a parent, I am sure you can relate. The difference between the child who authentically is sorry versus the one who just says sorry because you told them to do it, is generally pretty obvious. Maybe you can relate to this application yourself from a time when you were a child. I know there were many times my mom told me to say, "I am sorry," when in reality I would do the same thing again, given the chance.

Saying, "I am sorry," and meaning it from the heart is one of the beginning steps of reconciliation when it comes to wrongs or trespasses. Reconciliation is a financial term. It has to do with accounting and making sure all debts and credits are equal and the end result is a zero balance. Obviously, it can get more complicated than that, but that is the basic gist of it. As we start to link this aspect of debt and reconciliation, we can soon start to see how God's plan is that we have this reconciliation with Him first as well as with others in our life.

Since we are walking through Matthew, let me point out a few verses earlier in the book of Matthew that deal with repentance.

- *"Repent, for the kingdom of heaven is at hand."* Matthew 3:2
- *"Bear fruit in keeping with repentance."* Matthew 3:8

- *"I baptize you with water for repentance, but he who is coming after me is mightier than I, whose sandals I am not worthy to carry. He will baptize you with the Holy Spirit and fire."* Matthew 3:11
- *"From that time Jesus began to preach, saying, 'Repent, for the kingdom of heaven is at hand.'"* Matthew 4:17

Here are some verses after Matthew 6 that deal with repentance.

- *"Then he began to denounce the cities where most of his mighty works had been done, because they did not repent."* Matthew 11:20
- *"Woe to you, Chorazin! Woe to you, Bethsaida! For if the mighty works done in you had been done in Tyre and Sidon, they would have repented long ago in sackcloth and ashes."* Matthew 11:21
- *"The men of Nineveh will rise up at the judgment with this generation and condemn it, for they repented at the preaching of Jonah, and behold, something greater than Jonah is here."* Matthew 12:41

Repentance is a big deal in the Bible. It is where the beginning of forgiveness starts. Here are more passages to reflect on regarding repentance.

- *"John appeared, baptizing in the wilderness and proclaiming a baptism of repentance for the forgiveness of sins."* Mark 1:4
- *"Repent therefore, and turn back, that your sins may be blotted out."* Acts 3:19
- *"And Peter said to them, 'Repent and be baptized every one of you in the name of Jesus Christ for the forgiveness of your sins, and you will receive the gift of the Holy Spirit.'"* Acts 2:38
- *"God exalted him [Jesus] at his right hand as Leader and Savior, to give repentance to Israel and forgiveness of sins."* Acts 5:31

- *"Repent, therefore, of this wickedness of yours, and pray to the Lord that, if possible, the intent of your heart may be forgiven you."* Acts 8:22

The point of all these passages is to connect the idea of forgiveness with the aspect of repentance. It is a pretty important connection. As we are walking through applying forgiveness as Jesus taught it in Matthew 6:14-15, it is important to have a solid understanding of our own forgiveness from God. That understanding generally comes from an understanding of our own mistakes and wrongs we have committed against God and against others. When we ask God to forgive us, or we repent of the sins or wrongs we have done, are we doing it like a child that really does not want to do it? Are we only walking through the process because we have been told to? God is faithful to forgive us when we approach Him with a genuine and authentic heart of repentance. In 1 John 1:9-10, we read, *"If we confess our sins, he is faithful and just to forgive us our sins and to cleanse us from all unrighteousness. If we say we have not sinned, we make him a liar, and his word is not in us."*

We have all sinned. Just like in the parable, when the man knew he could not repay his debt to the master, he pleaded for the master's mercy. Our sins against God cannot be repaid by our own self, this is why we need a Savior. This is why we need Jesus to pay for the debt through the blood He shed on the cross.

Take time to think about repentance in your own life. Have you truly repented of the sins you have committed against God? Is your list really long like mine? I could do only good things for the rest of my life and I still would not be able to make up for all the wrong I have done. Receiving forgiveness starts with recognizing the fact that we have done wrong. This can be applied to those in our home, community, and workplace, but the most important part we need to address is how it applies to God Himself.

In 2 Corinthians 7:10, Paul writes. *"For godly grief produces a repentance that leads to salvation without regret, whereas*

worldly grief produces death." Mourning and grieving over the sins we have committed against God are good things. God is pleased when we humble ourselves and come before Him asking for forgiveness.

HEAVENLY FORGIVENESS MODELED
DEVOTION #3 - PASTOR JOHN CARTER

We have walked through this aspect of forgiveness, comparing it to financial debt, and then we looked at how repentance plays a big part in our own forgiveness from God. Now, we will look at the application part of forgiveness, the actual modeling it out in our own lives. Let me warn you ahead of time, this is going to be tough, especially if you have been seriously hurt and have very painful memories of being hurt. Trying to do it in your own strength is not going to lead to a positive outcome. Let me encourage you to start this devotion by praying and asking God to give you the strength, through the Holy Spirit, to be able to walk through modeling His forgiveness to other people.

Today, we are going to look at James' teaching to correlate some important things Jesus is teaching us in Matthew. James says this when walking us through forgiveness. He uses a slightly different word, but it has the same implication. The word "mercy" is closely related to the aspect of forgiveness. James 2:8-13 says, *"If you really fulfill the royal law according to the Scripture, 'You shall love your neighbor as yourself,' you are doing well. But if you show partiality, you are committing sin and are convicted by the law as transgressors. For whoever keeps the whole law but fails in one point has become guilty of all of it. For he who said, 'Do not commit adultery,' also said, 'Do not murder.' If you do not commit adultery but do murder, you have become a transgressor of the law. So speak and so act as those who are to be judged under the law of liberty. For judgment is without mercy to one who has shown no mercy. Mercy triumphs over judgment."*

James really expounds on this idea of how to apply what may seem like an impossible statement. He starts off with the second greatest commandment given to mankind, *"Love your neighbor as yourself."* The way in which we treat others is very important to God. James commends his readers that if they are applying this aspect of loving your neighbor as yourself, *"You are doing well."* It is always nice and encouraging when we can say, "Good job," to other people. As you are reflecting on your own life, maybe you have already walked through some hard times and forgiveness. This may just be a refresher for you and maybe you can encourage others by sharing your story to encourage them to walk through it as well. If this is new for you, find a fellow believer and tell them some of the hurt you are walking through. Ask them to be an encourager and someone that will pray with you through it.

James continues to lay this important foundation that we are all transgressors of God's holy, *"royal law."* He is teaching this aspect of partiality. It is about how you would treat one person differently than you would treat another. James flat-out calls it a sin, but more importantly, God calls it a sin. Leviticus 19:15 says, *"You shall do no injustice in court. You shall not be partial to the poor or defer to the great, but in righteousness shall you judge your neighbor."* Deuteronomy 1:17 adds, *"You shall not be partial in judgment. You shall hear the small and the great alike. You shall not be intimidated by anyone, for the judgment is God's. And the case that is too hard for you, you shall bring to me, and I will hear it."*

I think God knows that we tend to be partial people, meaning we have people we like and people, well we do not get along easily with. God shows no partiality when it comes to the sinner. He has a single standard by which He judges, James refers to it as the *"royal law."* Paul teaches much about the Judge of this law.

- *"There will be tribulation and distress for every human being who does evil, the Jew first and also the Greek, but glory and honor and peace for everyone who does good, the Jew first and also the Greek. For God shows no partiality."* Romans 2:9-11

- *"Masters, do the same to them, and stop your threatening, knowing that he who is both their Master and yours is in heaven, and that there is no partiality with him."* Ephesians 6:9

Paul sets the standard that God, Jesus, and the Holy Spirit, will not be partial in their judgment against sin. James then moves on to teach us the applications. He says to speak and act as those who are under the *"law of liberty."* There is a two-part instruction, the way we speak and the way we act towards someone. They need to be rooted in this amazing *"law of liberty."* I will paraphrase his next verse: merciless judgment will come to the one who has shown no mercy. This last phrase is very much in line with what Jesus teaches us in Matthew 6:14-15. So, here is the application. When you stand before God, will you receive His amazing mercy and forgiveness because of the faith you have in the work at the cross, resurrection, and person of Jesus Christ? If you have received the Holy Spirit because of your faith in Jesus Christ, then you can walk in this *"law of liberty."* Since you have been forgiven such a great debt, God says you can also, through the power of God, forgive those who have wronged you on this Earth.

This application is very hard and you might say to me, "You have no clue what evil was done to me? You do not know my particular circumstance? How could you dare ask me to forgive such evil?" You are 100% right. I do not know every single person's hardships or evil that they have had to walk through. I have my own story of hardships that are, more than likely, completely different than yours. What I do know is this amazing mercy that I received from the Father through the person of Jesus. I know the love that was shown to me and the forgiveness that was given to me by the Father through the debt that Jesus paid on my behalf. Because I know that, I am asked to reciprocate or to model that forgiveness to others. I am not to show any kind of partiality in how I distribute this forgiveness. I am to love every neighbor as though it was me. I love that James adds this last phase, *"Mercy triumphs over judgment."* If you are in the t-shirt business, that is a t-shirt I would buy. It could be said,

"Forgiveness beats a grudge." You might even say it like this, "Love wins over hate."

As you seriously consider the subject of forgiveness, consider the practical application of these verses. Are you living out this forgiveness you have received from God? Are you holding a grudge against someone? Do you find yourself being partial to a certain person or group of people because of past pain? The application of heavenly forgiveness is to forgive the debts or trespasses others have committed against you just like God has forgiven you of your trespasses. This is a two-way street. Maybe you know you have done wrong to someone else, and you need to seek them out and apologize. Repent for the wrong you have done. This also means, that if someone has asked for forgiveness you do not withhold it.

DISINGENUOUS FORGIVENESS
DEVOTION #4 - PASTOR JOHN CARTER

If you are a parent, you can probably relate to this idea of false forgiveness. Previously, I used this illustration about how we have to sometimes instruct our children to seek forgiveness, most of the time from another sibling. Instinctively, we know when our children mean it versus when they are just saying it to please someone else. This aspect of forgiveness and repentance is compared to two different kinds of grief from Paul. He describes them in 2 Corinthians 7:9-10, ***"As it is, I rejoice, not because you were grieved, but because you were grieved into repenting. For you felt a godly grief, so that you suffered no loss through us. For godly grief produces a repentance that leads to salvation without regret, whereas worldly grief produces death."***

If you know the story of the church in Corinth, you understand a little of what Paul is walking the church through. To say the church was a mess is probably an understatement. They were struggling with division, sin, and the many influences of the world around them. The city of Corinth was a major trade route in the Roman Empire. It had a reputation of being a very carnal city and Paul is giving instructions to the church on how to seek after true repentance and forgiveness. Paul knew the issues of the carnal city and was well aware of the sins that permeated the surroundings of the believers in Corinth. I think we can clearly say that sin hurts. It causes pain and damage, whether you are the one committing the sin or the one to whom the sin is being done. It just flat-out hurts!

I love that Paul separates this aspect of grief into two distinct categories. He identifies that there is grief or repentance that is godly. In contrast to ***"godly grief,"*** he also identifies grief he calls ***"worldly."***

Have you ever considered there are different types of grief? Maybe if I say it like this it might resonate a little more. Have you ever recognized genuine and authentic apologies versus someone saying, "I am sorry" and they are apologetic simply because they got caught? This is what Paul is walking the church at Corinth through. It is what authentic and genuine repentance looks like. Paul continues to say this in 2 Corinthians 7:11-12 *"For see what earnestness this godly grief has produced in you, but also what eagerness to clear yourselves, what indignation, what fear, what longing, what zeal, what punishment! At every point you have proved yourselves innocent in the matter. So although I wrote to you, it was not for the sake of the one who did the wrong, nor for the sake of the one who suffered the wrong, but in order that your earnestness for us might be revealed to you in the sight of God."*

This is such a profound passage to dwell on. Paul is writing to people in Corinth that have done wrong. He identifies something that is astounding. The purpose of his corrective letter was not specifically for those who did wrong nor was it for those who were wronged. It was intended to be for the people who genuinely desired to please God. In other words, he is saying to the one who wronged someone that their repentance should be earnest or genuine. Likewise, to the one who had wrong done to them, their forgiveness would produce earnest forgiveness or authentic forgiveness. This aspect of authentic forgiveness is not something we often identify with or easily relate to. It is easy to identify the child who is not really sorry about the wrong they did, but it is a little harder to identify the child who is not genuine in their forgiveness.

I have personally had to walk through this in my own life. Knowing that I had things that were done to me that were wrong, I assumed that I had the right to choose when and how I forgave. I could even pretend to forgive, only to use it as a weapon later against the person. One of the common signs you might see with someone who has not actually forgiven, is that they bring it up again when it is convenient for them. In other words, do we use their past wrongs to conveniently discredit them? Do we distance ourselves from the person who did wrong? This is necessary at times when dealing with domestic abuse, especially when the perpetrator has not sought repentance. For the most part, do we offer forgiveness and choose not to associate with someone that has wronged us? This could be a sign of unauthentic forgiveness. Do you feel continued bitterness or frustration regarding someone you have forgiven? Maybe you have a similar situation. The forgiveness you offer is only to your benefit. You choose to give it and take it at your own will. In Paul's dealing with repentance in Corinth, I believe he also deals with forgiveness. If you will permit me to slightly paraphrase to illustrate the point: godly forgiveness leads to salvation without regret. Obviously, there is only One that can offer forgiveness that leads to salvation and that is God the Father through Jesus Christ. However, can you say that about the wrong done to you? Can you forgive without regret? The earnestness of the one who repents must also be matched by the earnestness of the one who forgives. This should reveal in us our desire to please God or mirror the forgiveness we received from the Father to others.

Let me close today with this passage in Psalms 103. If you have time I would encourage you to read the whole Psalm. It is amazing! I picked a small portion of this amazing passage to have you reflect on the amazing love and forgiveness the Almighty God offers us. He desires us to also offer it to others.

Psalm 103:9-12 says, *"He will not always chide [shout], nor will he keep his anger forever. He does not deal with us according to our sins, nor repay us according to our iniquities. For as high as the heavens are above the earth, so great is his steadfast love toward those who fear him; as far as the east is from the west, so far does he remove our transgressions from us."*

God's forgiveness is *"as far as the east is from the west!"* It is amazing to know that God has this amazing ability to forgive our sins against Him. As we examine this, listen to God. We need to pray that we live it out in our own lives.

AUTHENTIC JUDGEMENT
DEVOTION #5 - PASTOR JOHN CARTER

We have been walking through the different aspects of forgiveness. Maybe this week has been very encouraging to you. Maybe this has been a harder week for you. Maybe you intentionally decided to not read this week's devotions just because of the topic. I get it. When we talk about forgiveness, most of us will relate to one side (forgiveness) or the other (repentance) or maybe both of the conversation. We recognize our wrongs and seek to make amends, but maybe, we do not receive it from the person we desire to reconcile with. Maybe you want to forgive but you are waiting for the other person to seek repentance. Maybe you have forgiven them time and time again and the offender keeps on hurting you. How do you deal with these circumstances in life?

As we look at forgiveness, I find it really important to follow the model laid down by Jesus in Matthew chapter 18. Matthew 18:15-17 says, *"If your brother sins against you, go and tell him his fault, between you and him alone. If he listens to you, you have gained your brother. But if he does not listen, take one or two others along with you, that every charge may be established by the evidence of two or three witnesses. If he refuses to listen to them, tell it to the church. And if he refuses to listen even to the church, let him be to you as a Gentile and a tax collector."*

The first step to walking through the process of forgiveness and repentance is to deal with the offense one-on-one. This is probably one of the hardest things for people to do. We create so many reasons not to do this. We have so many excuses. What if he or she does not listen? What if he or she gets angry? Is it that big of a deal to me? What if they stop being my friend? I am sure you have your own reasons to not approach someone that has possibly hurt or sinned against you. All of these reasons are actually disobedience to what Jesus teaches. He clearly establishes that we are to approach individuals one-on-one. It is important to note that the passage says to keep it between you and the person alone. Often times, this is not how we approach forgiveness or repentance. We often find ourselves talking about it to every other person but the one who did the wrong. This creates division right from the start.

Jesus, recognizing our fear and not discrediting it, establishes the next step if the person does not listen. Jesus says, *"take one or two others along with you."* The purpose of this is to have a neutral party. The key word is neutral. It is their job to establish every charge or offense. In other words, you give up, any right to accuse. You share your side and let the other share their side with someone who is neutral. By neutral, I mean they do not have a bias. It is not like you bring your best friend to go confront someone else. You bring someone that has no "skin in the game." The purpose of this is to ensure that the actual offense can be determined. There are a lot of scenarios that this process can weed out. Maybe the accuser has overreacted and it needs to be addressed. Maybe there was not actually an offense and it is only a major misunderstanding. Maybe the offense is very serious and, by establishing its seriousness, you now have one or two additional advocates that can help you walk through the process. Jesus refers here to an Old Testament passage. Deuteronomy 19:15 says, *"A single witness shall not suffice against a person for any crime or for any wrong in connection with any offense that he has committed. Only on the evidence of two witnesses or of three witnesses shall a charge be established."*

It is a serious issue to bring a charge against someone. Jesus affirms this Old Testament law by establishing it to be something we adhere to in the New Testament. Paul, John, and the author of Hebrews, all taught this very law to the church. In your spare time, take a look at some of these cross-references (2 Corinthians 13:1; Numbers 35:30; John 8:17; 1 Timothy 5:19; Hebrews 10:28). The key word in all of this is "charge." Matthew and the book of Deuteronomy use the same word. The aspect of charging someone with a crime, a sin, or an offense needs to have the right process. It needs to be affirmed by two or three witnesses. We have seen this done poorly in the secular world and just as poorly in the church. When someone makes an accusation against someone else and it goes crazy in the media, it removes and destroys that person before the proper evidence can even be examined. Oftentimes, the accusation causes more damage and the accuser becomes the offender, the "false witness" in essence. The process of establishing the charge is a very important and crucial process of what Jesus teaches in forgiveness and repentance.

In the event that there are sufficient charges to be established by the witness of two or three and the offender has refused to repent, it is brought to the elders of the church. The elders of the church will address the issue with the individual and seek reconciliation. If the one accused chooses not to repent and walk in accordance with Scripture, then that individual is to be considered an unbeliever. The hope is that it never reaches this point. The desire would be godly repentance and reconciliation prior to this process; but in some extreme and difficult situations, the church elders have to walk through these difficult decisions. This is one reason why we are asked to pray for our elders in Hebrews 13:18-19.

What is amazing about this passage, is right after Jesus teaches this process to His disciples, Peter has a question. Matthew 18:21-22 records, *"Then Peter came up and said to him, 'Lord, how often will my brother sin against me, and I forgive him? As many as seven times?' Jesus said to him, 'I do not say to you seven times, but seventy-seven times.'"*

Maybe you have asked yourself, "How many times am I going to have to forgive this person for the same thing?" Let me flip it a little bit, "How many times have you had to approach God to forgive you for the same sin?" Jesus' response is befitting His character and behavior. Peter thinks he is probably being very spiritual by offering forgiveness seven times. The number seven seems like a lot of times to forgive someone that has wronged you. If I am being honest, I would struggle if someone came to me seven times to ask for forgiveness. I would seriously question if it is serious or authentic. Jesus says to do it 77 times. He expresses a number that seems so wild and far-fetched you seriously have to ask, "Jesus, are you for real saying 77 times?" We may even be shaking our heads like no way. While this passage may seem very overwhelming, it also shows the amazing love and forgiveness that God offers each and every one of us. God wants us to mimic His behavior. He is not going to tell us to do something He Himself would not do. When he tells Peter to do it 77 times, He is actually showing us His immense desire to offer us forgiveness. When we receive and understand His forgiveness for us, it is so we are able to mimic that towards others.

Take some time today to praise God for His amazing love and forgiveness toward us! Maybe you need to mimic this behavior of God's love and forgiveness toward someone else. Pray about it, then live it out!

DOERS VS. HEARERS

DEVOTION #6 - PASTOR JOHN CARTER

As we conclude our week on forgiveness, I am reminded of the passage in James that deals with those who are *"hearers only"* versus those who live it out. Forgiveness is a hard subject to truly live out. Hurt, pain, betrayal, neglect, abuse, suffering, and sin are what we are talking about forgiving. I have said this before, sin is ugly! Forgiving sin against us is a very hard thing to do. This week has been a serious challenge for me as I have been writing these devotions. Forgiveness is so hard because we feel the wounds and scars. Sometimes, we are so blinded by the scar and wounds we forget that hanging onto vengeance equally produces scars and wounds in ourselves.

James 1:19-22 says, *"Know this, my beloved brothers: let every person be quick to hear, slow to speak, slow to anger; for the anger of man does not produce the righteousness of God. Therefore put away all filthiness and rampant wickedness and receive with meekness the implanted word, which is able to save your souls. But be doers of the word, and not hearers only, deceiving yourselves."*

I love the book of James! It is just so practical in so many ways. My initial response to the wrong done to me is retaliation and anger. I have more of the "fight" response than I do of the "flight" response. I do not say this as a good thing. I have, in many cases, done more damage than good because of my fight response. In fact, James is very clear that *"the anger of man does not produce the righteousness of God."* I would definitely second that sentiment in my own life. This week we have looked at a lot of passages that teach us the different aspects of forgiveness and repentance. The fundamental question is will you be a *"doer"* or will you be just a *"hearer"*? I am sure if you have been around church any number of times, you have heard that holding onto bitterness will do more damage than good to you. James teaches us this in the form of deceiving ourselves. He says to not deceive yourself by just hearing the Word of God. Understanding a concept is different than living it out. Today's devotion is going to be pretty straightforward. Are we going to live out the things the Holy Spirit has pointed out to us? Will we continue to deceive ourselves?

Have you ever asked yourself, "What does it mean to be a *'doer'* of the Word?" James continues a little farther down and tells us in James 1:25, ***"But the one who looks into the perfect law, the law of liberty, and perseveres, being no hearer who forgets but a doer who acts, he will be blessed in his doing."***

The doer acts. It is very practical and very precise! It leaves very little room to navigate away from it. James points to this amazing ***"law of liberty"*** that we receive in the Living Word, the person of Jesus Christ. Jesus is the One who took on all our sins as a perfect and sinless man. He is truly the One who by all rights could hold a grudge, rightfully condemn, and have every right to be angry. James points us to know Him first. If you are struggling with this week's topic of forgiveness, can I encourage you to rest in the person of Jesus? Ask Him to help you, to walk with you as you try to live out God's instructions and commandments in your life. James does not leave us without hope of blessing. The one who chooses to act, the doer of the Word of God, is affirmed by James that there is a blessing in it. This blessing may look different for each person. In regards to forgiveness, the blessing may mean healing from a wound you have had for decades. Maybe the hurt you have been carrying and festering will start healing. Maybe it will be a genuine and powerful reconciliation. Maybe it will be knowing you are forgiven, not only by God, but by the persons you have wronged. I do not know how walking through repentance and forgiveness will bless you. What I do know is, if you choose to not act on it, it will manifest itself.

I am not a big fan of writing out my prayers to God, but as I am writing this devotion I feel God leading me to do this. I feel that this may be something useful or encouraging to you, the reader.

Please take time to join me in prayer as we conclude this devotion, earnestly seek after God, and live out what He has asked us to do.

Dear Father in Heaven,

Thank you for loving me! Thank you for the amazing forgiveness you offer to me! God, I know it is not easy for you to keep hearing me make mistakes. You desire for me to be an example of your love and forgiveness to others. It is really hard sometimes to do that. I cannot help but feel the pain and see the damage that has been done to me. I feel often very selfish that I have not even considered the pain and damage done to you. Lord, please forgive me for this. I desire to walk after you and your righteousness. Please help me to do the things you have commanded me to do. Help me be a doer, so that through me, others will taste your goodness and love. Jesus, thank you for carrying my sins to the cross. I know your love for me is real. As I do my best to walk through forgiving others, Jesus, please remind me over and over again how much you have forgiven me. I love you!

In Jesus' name, Amen.

LESSON SEVEN

Fasting

PASTOR CHUCK LINDSEY

"Moreover, when you fast, do not be like the hypocrites, with a sad countenance. For they disfigure their faces that they may appear to men to be fasting. Assuredly, I say to you, they have their reward. But you, when you fast, anoint your head and wash your face, so that you do not appear to men to be fasting, but to your Father who is in the secret place; and your Father who sees in secret will reward you openly." Matthew 6:16-18 (NKJV)

1. What comes to mind when you think of fasting?

    "giving up" something - food, internet, anything to get clarity from God. Denying self of something

2. Have you ever fasted? How long? Why?

    No I have.

We turn now from forgiveness to the topic of fasting. What is fasting? **"_Fast_"** comes from the Greek word "nesteuo" and means "to abstain from food or drink."

In a biblical sense, it is always for spiritual reasons. In other words, biblical fasting is not a dietary or cleansing practice. It is a denial of self. It is a denial of what the physical body demands. The desires of the physical are denied, refused, and abstained from for the purpose of focusing all attention on the spiritual. In the Bible, we regularly see the denial of food for a determined period of time to subsequently focus on prayer. Biblically, fasting is often unplanned and is a reaction to some tragic news or heavy situation. It is like the spiritual need eclipses the physical. That is a reactive form of fasting that follows trouble. This is not the kind of fasting that Jesus is speaking about here in verses 16-18.

3. Do you remember a time when you could not eat and just focused on prayer?

yes -

The kind of fasting Jesus teaches about in these verses is planned. It is not, "If tragedy strikes and you go into mourning and fasting, do it this way." It is, "When you determine to fast, do it like this." Notice that Jesus assumes that we as humans will fast. He does not say "if," He says, **"when."** Jesus assumes that we will recognize when there are times in life when we need to hit the pause button in life and turn our attention to the eternal. He assumes that we will recognize a "leanness of soul," a lack, or a need that cannot be satisfied otherwise and that this will cause us to purposefully deny the physical to give our undivided attention to the spiritual and eternal. However, in our busy society, with so much vying for our attention, we are rarely, if ever, aware of this leanness that would push us to **"_fast_."** Fasting is an effort to fix this need of the soul and the spiritual hunger we can no longer live with.

4. Should fasting be a regular practice today? Why or why not? How often? How long?

I'm learning it should – Too many life distractions

The fact that fasting is associated with a spiritual lack is seen in something the disciples of John and the Pharisees said to Jesus. In Matthew 9:14 (NKJV), they asked, **"Why do we and the Pharisees fast often, but Your disciples do not fast?"** The disciples of John and the Pharisees were regularly, as a part of their discipleship, denying food and drink. Jesus and His disciples were not doing this. They were always eating together and with others. John's disciples and the Pharisees asked, **"Why?"** The answer was of course that Jesus' disciples had the One who provides right there with them. Psalm 145:16 (NKJV) says, **"You open Your hand and satisfy the** *desire of every living thing."* They walked with, talked with, and slept next to the One who fills up the soul. When they were "lean," they could lean towards Him, hear His words, and be filled to the full. There was no need to fast, He was right there. This was Jesus' answer to them. He said, *"Can the friends of the bridegroom mourn as long as the bridegroom is with them?"* What was Jesus' point? He was right there with them! They could have what fasting brings simply by being near Him. However, He went on to say that once He was gone, then they would *"fast"* (Matthew 9:15, NKJV).

5.   What are some other ways to be near God without fasting?

Prayer, in the word, Fellowship, serving

So, *"when"* we *"fast,"* we are to *"not be* like the hypocrites." *"Be"* comes from the Greek verb "ginomai" and means "to make or become."

Jesus warns us again of these mask-wearers or pretenders. "Do not follow their example," He says. The warning here is against outward or external fasting. Fasting is to be a private matter, something that is between God and me. Everything the *"hypocrites"* (religious leaders) did was to be "seen" by others. As with their praying and their giving, they fasted so that they would be seen. Jesus says here their goal was to *"appear"* spiritual, closer to God, and generally more than others. *"Appear"* comes from the Greek word "phaino" and means "to be seen as."

6.   How can it be good for someone else to know you are fasting?

Accountability - support, encouragement, them praying for me.

7. How can it be dangerous for others to know you are fasting?

becoming prideful

The religious leaders wanted people to know that they were fasting. They wanted others to see it and admire them for their spiritual dedication and sacrifice. To this end, they would go as far as to **"_disfigure_"** their faces. **"_Disfigure_"** comes from the Greek word "aphanizo" and means "to ruin the natural appearance."

The religious leaders would comically apply makeup to their faces and allow their countenance to sag and droop so that they would **"_appear_"** to be starving. How ironic this is! While pretending to be physically starving, the leanness was actually in their own souls! Jesus concludes the warning with the words, **"Assuredly, I say to you, they have their reward."**

8. Why is drawing attention to ourselves dangerous?

Pride - Glory of men + not God

"_Have_" comes from the Greek verb "apecho" and means "to hold in place." It is a word that was used to describe a boat being docked away from the shore. The idea here is that they have chosen their reward - the admiration of people. Jesus says it is a reward that does not come close to "shore." It is a reward that falls short and does not last. They foolishly held themselves back from what they could have had - the reward from God which endures forever.

9. What is the reward from God?

In verses 17-18, our Lord moves from the negative to the positive in His instruction on this topic, "do not do this" to "do it this way." He says, *"But you, when you fast, anoint your head and wash your face, so that you do not appear to men to be fasting."*

"Anoint" comes from the Greek verb "aleipho" and means "to cover over or rub into." Jesus essentially says, "Wash yourself, anoint your face (with oil) so that you appear to be healthy" or normal. The goal here is to conceal what is being done rather than to display it. Again, it is to be between the Lord and me. He *"sees."*

"Sees" comes from the Greek verb "blepo" and means "to watch or see as it happens."

Jesus assures us of this with the words, *"But to your Father who is in the secret place; and your Father who sees in secret will reward you openly."* Once again, the promise is that as we conceal the matter now from men, we will be rewarded openly one day by Him. He is reasoning with us and we are encouraged to make the wise choice.

Jesus is basically saying, "When you set time aside to specifically focus on the spiritual rather than the physical, do not be like those who do it to be seen and admired by others. That is a paltry reward. Do not appear to be fasting at all. Just do this before your Father who sees all and He will reward you!"

NOTES

Philippians 4:4
Psalm 51
Ezekiel 11

FASTING

DEVOTION #1 - PASTOR JOHN CARTER

As we continue in Matthew chapter 6, we see Jesus teach us aspects of fasting. Fasting is an interesting Bible concept that has been present throughout all the Scriptures. However, it is possible that you know very little about this subject. This is why we will study it and hopefully learn the proper way to walk through fasting and how to properly apply it to our lives. So, this week, we are going to study the concept of fasting.

Matthew 6:16-18 says, *"And when you fast, do not look gloomy like the hypocrites, for they disfigure their faces that their fasting may be seen by others. Truly, I say to you, they have received their reward. But when you fast, anoint your head and wash your face, that your fasting may not be seen by others but by your Father who is in secret. And your Father who sees in secret will reward you."*

If you have been following us through this series in Matthew, you will quickly identify Jesus' similar teaching style of comparing hypocrites against authentic followers and worshipers of God. In previous weeks, we have seen this comparison in how we give, how we pray, and now, in how we fast.

What do you understand about fasting? Maybe some of you think of the Catholic observation of Lent prior to Easter. Maybe you think of the "Daniel Fast" as a type of diet. Maybe you are familiar with this aspect of fasting a daily meal for the purpose of bodybuilding. The truth is that when it comes to fasting, there seem to be a lot of different ideas about it. Jesus clearly teaches that fasting is something we should be doing. He says, *"When you fast,"* and the implication is that we would do this fasting at some point in our walk with Christ. The difference in when to do it is pretty dramatic. The word *"when"* implies that you will participate at some point in the future, in contrast to the word "if" which leaves the door open to the idea you may never participate. Maybe you are a new Christian and you have never fasted before, I do not want you to freak out. As we walk through understanding the element of worship that takes place in fasting, you will find yourself (hopefully) excited to participate in His amazing way to worship and have communion with God.

Isaiah chapter 58 is a good place to start as we begin to walk through fasting. This is a chapter that shows us many of the serious aspects of fasting. The house of Jacob had a question and received a response to how they approached fasting. Isaiah 58:3 says, **"'Why have we fasted, and you see it not? Why have we humbled ourselves, and you take no knowledge of it?' Behold, in the day of your fast you seek your own pleasure, and oppress all your workers."**

Some of the initial understanding we can gain from this passage is that fasting is an act of humbling oneself. This is where we will lay the foundation. This fasting is not for some form of personal gain, whether it be for Lent, a diet, or for a healthier body. It is important to understand the biblical reason is to be humble before God. It is to represent how we show God our humility towards him. In the same passage, we see that the house of Jacob did not understand why God did not see their false humility; He did not acknowledge it. The response was that the people (house of Jacob) were doing it for their own pleasure. They had really bad motives behind their fasting. They did it to oppress their workers.

As we study this topic, we should start by truly seeking to humbly walk in line with what God designed. It is not about giving up something for a short period of time to feel good about yourself, nor is meant to be a diet so you lose weight. It was not designed to be a way to gain health. It was meant to be a way to show God our humility before His very eyes.

Fasting is recorded in Isaiah as the true design and heart of God.

Isaiah 58:6-7 continues, *"Is not this the fast that I choose: to loose the bonds of wickedness, to undo the straps of the yoke, to let the oppressed go free, and to break every yoke? Is it not to share your bread with the hungry and bring the homeless poor into your house; when you see the naked, to cover him, and not to hide yourself from your own flesh?"*

Wow, that is a completely different idea of fasting than what is commonly discussed! Instead of just temporarily giving up a meal, God asks you to take the food you would have eaten and give it to the hungry. God directs that during your fast, you would give the food you had not eaten to the homeless in your town. If you see someone without covering, you would give up your covering for their benefit. This is really and truly the heart of fasting.

We often associate fasting as some form of giving up on our part and we hope that God will see us for our sacrifice. Just as the house of Jacob was confused about their fasting, I think we in this day and age are equally confused. The condemnation of the house of Jacob was that their workers were oppressed. Isaiah describes their oppression in verses 6-7. They think they are acting humbly by going without food; however, they completely ignore the hungry. Maybe they stop watching T.V. for 40 days, but completely walk past the homeless that have no place to warm their hands. Maybe they give up buying the new Jordans, but walk past those who have no shoes on their feet.

I know this is a harsh opening to fasting. It is convicting me as I write it. However, I would rather be convicted and understand how God desires me to worship Him, than continue to do something in vain. Today, take a deep breath and ask God to open your heart to fasting and how it is to be applied to your life. Ask the Holy Spirit to teach you to understand fasting as God designed it.

THE WHAT AND WHY OF FASTING
DEVOTION #2 - PASTOR JOHN CARTER

There are two important questions to ask when it comes to fasting. What exactly is fasting? For what purpose do we engage in it? As we mentioned yesterday, there may be many different characteristics of fasting that we have added over the years like a personal sacrifice, abstaining from something like technology, and not eating. We also see the use of fasting for health purposes like cleansing, losing weight, and personal accomplishments. As I try to do my best to walk through the biblical definition of what fasting is and why we do it, please keep in mind that this is only a short devotion. It may require some research beyond this.

Fasting, in its conventional understanding, is to abstain from certain foods, for a religious purpose. As we look at some examples of fasting in the Bible, we start to see what God desires from us through fasting.

Fasting is an expression of mourning.

- *"Then all the people of Israel, the whole army, went up and came to Bethel and wept. They sat there before the Lord and fasted that day until evening, and offered burnt offerings and peace offerings before the Lord."* Judges 20:26

- *"And they took their bones and buried them under the tamarisk tree in Jabesh and fasted seven days."* 1 Samuel 31:13

Fasting is an expression of repentance.

- *"So they gathered at Mizpah and drew water and poured it out before the Lord and fasted on that day and said there,*

'We have sinned against the Lord.' And Samuel judged the people of Israel at Mizpah." 1 Samuel 7:6

- *"And it shall be a statute to you forever that in the seventh month, on the tenth day of the month, you shall afflict yourselves and shall do no work, either the native or the stranger who sojourns among you. For on this day shall atonement be made for you to cleanse you. You shall be clean before the Lord from all your sins."* Leviticus 16:29-30

Fasting is an expression of seeking God.

- *"David therefore sought God on behalf of the child. And David fasted and went in and lay all night on the ground. And the elders of his house stood beside him, to raise him from the ground, but he would not, nor did he eat food with them."* 2 Samuel 12:16-17

- *"Then his servants said to him, 'What is this thing that you have done? You fasted and wept for the child while he was alive; but when the child died, you arose and ate food.' He said, 'While the child was still alive, I fasted and wept, for I said, 'Who knows whether the Lord will be gracious to me, that the child may live?' But now he is dead. Why should I fast? Can I bring him back again? I shall go to him, but he will not return to me.'"* 2 Samuel 12:21-23

Fasting is an expression of seeking God's protection.

- *"Then I proclaimed a fast there, at the river Ahava, that we might humble ourselves before our God, to seek from him a safe journey for ourselves, our children, and all our goods."* Ezra 8:21

- *"So we fasted and implored our God for this, and he listened to our entreaty."* Ezra 8:23

Fasting is an expression of loving your neighbor.

- *"Is not this the fast that I [God] choose: to loose the bonds of wickedness, to undo the straps of the yoke, to let the oppressed go free, and to break every yoke? Is it not to share your bread with the hungry and bring the homeless poor into your house; when you see the naked, to cover him, and not to hide yourself from your own flesh [family or seed]?"* Isaiah 58:6-7

Fasting is an expression of prayer.

- *"Cry aloud; do not hold back; lift up your voice like a trumpet; declare to my people their transgression, to the house of Jacob their sins. Yet they seek me daily and delight to know my ways, as if they were a nation that did righteousness and did not forsake the judgment of their God; they ask of me righteous judgments; they delight to draw near to God."* Isaiah 58:1-2

- *"As soon as I heard these words I sat down and wept and mourned for days, and I continued fasting and praying before the God of heaven."* Nehemiah 1:4

So, back to the questions, what is fasting and why do we do it? I would contend that fasting is the humbling of oneself before God by enduring an affliction or abstaining from food for the purpose of seeking Him so that one can repent, inquire, mourn (seek comfort), petition, and request God to hear them regarding particular issue.

When we fast to please and worship God, there is a promise that Isaiah wrote for us. The promise of God is to hear us when we call, mourn, and cry. He will comfort us with His words, *"Here I am."* He will guide, heal, and protect us. If you are familiar with military terms, God literally says He "has your six." In this devotion, it is very hard to walk through every element of fasting. I hope I was able to give you at least a basic foundation for what fasting is and why it is so important for us. We know Jesus fasted (Matthew 4:1-9; Luke 4:1-2) and the early church fathers fasted (Acts 13:1-3; Acts 14:21-23). So, it is important that we walk in accordance with the Word of God when we fast. Having a good solid understanding and purpose for it is crucial for us today. There are many alternative reasons to fast in today's age (which are not bad); but if we approach biblical fasting with some of these understandings, we may not fully grasp the major importance of fasting for our walk with Christ.

Isaiah 58:8-14 says, *"Then shall your light break forth like the dawn, and your healing shall spring up speedily; your righteousness shall go before you; the glory of the Lord shall be your rear guard. Then you shall call, and the Lord will answer; you shall cry, and he will say, 'Here I am.' If you take away the yoke from your midst, the pointing of the finger, and speaking wickedness, if you pour yourself out for the hungry and satisfy the desire of the afflicted, then shall your light rise in the darkness and your gloom be as the noonday. And the Lord will guide you continually and satisfy your desire in scorched places and make your bones strong; and you shall be like a watered garden, like a spring of water, whose waters do not fail. And your ancient ruins shall be rebuilt; you shall raise up the foundations of many generations; you shall be called the repairer of the breach, the restorer of streets to dwell in. If you turn back your foot from the Sabbath, from doing your pleasure on my holy day, and call the Sabbath a delight and the holy day of the Lord honorable; if you honor it, not going your own ways, or seeking your own pleasure, or talking idly; then you shall take delight in the Lord, and I will make you ride on the heights of the earth; I will feed you with the heritage of Jacob your father, for the mouth of the Lord has spoken."*

DISFIGURED FASTING - ASCETICISM
DEVOTION #3 - PASTOR JOHN CARTER

"And when you fast, do not look gloomy like the hypocrites, for they disfigure their faces that their fasting may be seen by others. Truly, I say to you, they have received their reward."
Matthew 6:16

Apparently, there were some people who decided to fast so others would see them. Personally, I am not sure what good this did for anybody. They would disfigure themselves, for what purpose? Did they want to appear righteous? Were they hoping to receive some form of praise? It is a little bewildering for me to consider the gain that comes from doing this especially when I link it to fasting. Please do not take this the wrong way, but I am not going to give up food so you think more highly of me. I need food and to think that disfiguring myself in any way would bring praise or honor to God seems crazy.

As crazy as it sounds, Paul had to deal with others as well. Colossians 2:18-19 says, *"Let no one disqualify you, insisting on asceticism and worship of angels, going on in detail about visions, puffed up without reason by his sensuous mind, and not holding fast to the Head, from whom the whole body, nourished and knit together through its joints and ligaments, grows with a growth that is from God."*

The word *"asceticism"* as defined by Webster's Dictionary, is "the practice of strict self-denial as a measure of personal and especially spiritual discipline: the condition, practice, or mode of life of an ascetic: rigorous abstention from self-indulgence."

The Greek word used here in its basic form means humility. The word is used to describe true and honest humility in contrast to vain humility. This is the same word used in Philippians 2:3, *"Do nothing from selfish ambition or conceit, but in humility count others more significant than yourselves."*

Since Greek is a precise language, we can differentiate the intended use from Colossians as to Philippians. In other words, one is a genuine and authentic humility versus a vain or disingenuous humility.

As we read Matthew chapter 6 and listen to what Jesus is teaching regarding fasting, we need to seriously consider how we choose to humble ourselves. Looking back at yesterday's definition of fasting, we see humility as a major component of fasting. We can have a false or dishonest approach to our motives when we fast. In Matthew chapter 6, we see Jesus warning about dishonest humility in fasting, for the purpose of others seeing us.

Jesus notes that their reward has been received. Honestly, after looking through the amazing promise that comes from walking in true, authentic humility before God, it is amazing to me that anyone would even want to trade the promises of God for cheap recognition.

Why would you want to give the promises of God away? They are promises of hearing, comforting, protecting, guiding, and healing us. If we could realize this, we might have less disfiguring happening in our current culture, as we are a particularly vain culture. Everyone wants to be seen. Disingenuous humility is definitely a thing we see. It is even in the church. We may talk about how we are fasting and think nothing of the implication. Zechariah 7:4-6 should help us with the right heart to approach our fasting that we do in secret, *"Then the word of the Lord of hosts came to me: 'Say to all the people of the land and the priests, 'When you fasted and mourned in the fifth month and in the seventh, for these seventy years, was it for me that you fasted? And when you eat and when you drink, do you not eat for yourselves and drink for yourselves?'"*

God asks a fundamental question, "Was it for Me that you fasted?" This is one of the most important questions I believe we need to walk through when choosing to fast. Are you doing it for God? Is it a genuine aspect of humbling yourself before God? If you tend to find yourself answering those questions with a negative response, do not do it. Do not fast. Get your heart right and do not walk into fasting as a casual thing to just do for fun. God is not pleased with our halfhearted efforts. We see this in Malachi 1:8-9, *"When you offer blind animals in sacrifice, is that not evil? And when you offer those that are lame or sick, is that not evil? Present that to your governor; will he accept you or show you favor? says the Lord of hosts. And now entreat the favor of God, that he may be gracious to us. With such a gift from your hand, will he show favor to any of you? says the Lord of hosts."*

The whole point is, do not do something disingenuously or half-heartedly. Be authentic and genuine in your humility and sacrifice to God. He finds favor in this. The other aspect that we need to mention is our heart towards others when we fast. In Zachariah, we examined God's question, "Did you do this for me?" Just a few short verses later, Zechariah 7:8-10 says, *"And the word of the Lord came to Zechariah, saying, 'Thus says the Lord of hosts, Render true judgments, show kindness and mercy to one another, do not oppress the widow, the fatherless, the sojourner, or the poor, and let none of you devise evil against another in your heart.'"*

I find this interesting that God recognizes our human character. When we are hungry, we tend to be unkind or show very little mercy to others. I think there is a Snickers commercial that represents this aspect pretty well. The diva or "hangry" person changes the way they treat people around them as soon as they consume a candy bar. I love that God, knowing our own character as humans, is kind enough to warn us not to pay attention to others around us, even when we fast. What good is it if we fast with a serious heart toward God but ignore our neighbors as we do it? In Zechariah, the poor, widowed, fatherless, and even the intentions of your heart towards your brother, require your examination.

Matthew 22:36-40 addresses this, ***"'Teacher, which is the great commandment in the Law?' And he said to him, 'You shall love the Lord your God with all your heart and with all your soul and with all your mind. This is the great and first commandment. And a second is like it: You shall love your neighbor as yourself. On these two commandments depend all the Law and the Prophets.'"***

Jesus summarizes the whole Old Testament to these fundamental principles. I am hoping you can see the link from Zachariah mentioning fasting to how Jesus talks about it in Matthew chapter 6. First, we need to make sure we are fasting with a genuine heart of worship for God. Second, we cannot make it about ourselves. Third, we cannot forget to love our neighbor while we do it.

Fasting with a genuinely humble heart is what God desires for us. Praying and fasting go together. As you think about fasting, start by asking God to work on your heart. Ask Him to show you aspects of your life that may not be so humble. Ask God to teach you how to love Him more. Evaluate how you can love others around you a little better.

ANOINTING AND WASHING IN FASTING
DEVOTION #4 - PASTOR JOHN CARTER

Matthew 6:17-18 *"But when you fast, anoint your head and wash your face, that your fasting may not be seen by others but by your Father who is in secret. And your Father who sees in secret will reward you."*

As Jesus continued to teach about fasting, we see Him give this instruction regarding the anointing of your head and the washing of your face. There is another passage of Scripture that shows this in a practical sense. Let us look at what Jesus might be referring to in 2 Samuel 12:16, *"David therefore sought God on behalf of the child. And David fasted and went in and lay all night on the ground."*

When the unfortunate news of the death of his child comes, we see David's response in 2 Samuel 12:19-20, *"But when David saw that his servants were whispering together, David understood that the child was dead. And David said to his servants, 'Is the child dead?' They said, 'He is dead.' Then David arose from the earth and washed and anointed himself and changed his clothes. And he went into the house of the Lord and worshiped. He then went to his own house. And when he asked, they set food before him, and he ate."*

If you read the full chapter, you will see that David is fasting to plead with God for the life of his child. David falls to the ground and does not move, eat, or bathe for seven days. He earnestly pleads with God. According to God's wisdom, for reasons we cannot understand, the child does not survive. When David understands this, the first thing he does is to go and clean up. He washes and anoints his head.

What can we glean from these two passages regarding the instruction Jesus gives us? It helps to look at David's words to his servants who were confused by his actions. David tells them in 2 Samuel 12:22-23, *"He said, 'While the child was still alive, I fasted and wept, for I said, 'Who knows whether the Lord will be gracious to me, that the child may live?' But now he is dead. Why should I fast? Can I bring him back again? I shall go to him, but he will not return to me.'"*

David clearly communicated his motive for fasting and what he hoped for. Whatever the reason might be, God choose to bring the child to Himself. I love that David understood this and articulates that, one day, they will be together. He is aware of the fact that the child is with God and he will one day see his beloved child with God.

We see some incredible things in the example of David.

1. He boldly approached the Father with his pleas.
2. He accepted the answer that God gave him.
3. He moved forward and was not loathing in self-pity.

I feel like David could have easily gotten up from those seven days and made a huge scene about how God did not listen to him, how he sacrificed so much, and yet, God did not allow things to happen the way he wanted them to. David could have walked before other people and said how he had fasted, made everyone aware of the situation and the sadness that took place, then easily turned it into a conversation about himself. As narcissistic as that would have been, we do not see David doing that. He got up, cleaned up, and anointed himself. He humbled himself before God, and accepted the will of the Father.

When Jesus instructs us to wash and anoint ourselves (Matthew 6), He is reaffirming the previous message that your reason for fasting is not for others to see. He wants it to be something we do out of earnestly seeking God. He wants it to be something we do out of a genuine heart of worship. When we go back and look at some of the reasons people fasted in the Bible (mourning, repentance, seeking God, desiring God's protection, loving your neighbor, prayer), one thing becomes abundantly clear, God is the one with the authority and power. When we approach a God that has all the wisdom, understanding, and knowledge of all situations, do we trust His decisions? Will we be obedient to His will? As Jesus teaches and instructs us on fasting, He keeps drawing us back to the character and power of the Father. He is the one who sees in secret. He is the one who knows and understands. He knows what we do not know. So as we fast, for whatever reason we are fasting, do we see it as a way to get what we want (an extra step to a genie in a bottle) or do we submit to God and trust Him for every possible answer or outcome?

The anointing and washing are other ways to show that we trust God and that His answer is the best one. It really comes back to an act of worship, even if the answer is not the one we desired. We choose to not make it about us, but lean back on the will of the Father. Just like we learned from the Lord's prayer in Matthew 6:10, *"Your kingdom come, your will be done, on earth as it is in heaven."*

If this is our genuine and authentic desire in our prayer, it should also be our genuine and authentic desire when we fast. This is why you see the same warning when it comes to prayer as you do with fasting. Do not do it before men that can see for personal praise, but do it in secret before God who sees in secret. It is in the secret acknowledgment that we trust God's decision over our own will so that the Father will reward us. This reward is not always given to us in the manner by which we expect or the answer we hope for.

REWARDS OF FASTING IN SECRET
DEVOTION #5 - PASTOR JOHN CARTER

Matthew 6:17-18 *"But when you fast, anoint your head and wash your face, that your fasting may not be seen by others but by your Father who is in secret. And your Father who sees in secret will reward you."*

My hope and prayer is that, as you have been reading this week on fasting, you are a little more aware of the role fasting plays in worshiping God. God links the way we give, pray, and fast as ways we worship Him. It is pleasing to God when we do these things according to His will and in secret. He is happy with us when our motives in seeking Him, talking to Him, and blessing others, are genuine and authentic.

Does secret fasting produce a better result? Luke 18:9-12 says, *"He also told this parable to some who trusted in themselves that they were righteous, and treated others with contempt: 'Two men went up into the temple to pray, one a Pharisee and the other a tax collector. The Pharisee, standing by himself, prayed thus: 'God, I thank you that I am not like other men, extortioners, unjust, adulterers, or even like this tax collector. I fast twice a week; I give tithes of all that I get.'"*

We can feel the pretentiousness of this person right from the get-go. We can really see what Jesus was referencing when He talked about people who fasted for others to see their righteous deeds. It is interesting that this Pharisee thought his routine of fasting two times a week somehow gave him superiority over someone else. In this passage, the key aspect is described early on. He trusted in himself to obtain his own righteousness. This is a huge issue to talk through. I think it fits nicely in our conversation about fasting, because fasting is about humbling oneself. We really need to see how Jesus describes what it means to humble oneself. Obviously, in the example of the Pharisee, we see his lack of humility; yet, the Pharisee thought he was totally there. Why would God not reward him for all of his good behavior and righteous deeds? It is really important we do not walk in denial of the Good News of Jesus Christ. Luke 18:13-14 continues, *"But the tax collector, standing far off, would not even lift up his eyes to heaven, but beat his breast, saying, 'God, be merciful to me, a sinner!' I tell you, this man went down to his house justified, rather than the other. For everyone who exalts himself will be humbled, but the one who humbles himself will be exalted."*

The theme this whole week is really centered around humility. Yes, we are talking about fasting; however, the core of it all is humility. Jesus informs us through these words in Luke that our justification before God the Father is directly rooted in our understanding of humility. The contrast is very clear. The tax collector approaches God with complete humility. He sees God as one to fear (*"standing far off"*), as one who has the authority to give out righteous judgment (*"would not even lift up his eyes to heaven"*), and as one who could rightfully condemn the tax collector (*"beat his breast"*).

There is a lot displayed by the tax collector in this story Jesus shares with us. First, is the approach to the way in which the tax collector came to God. He recognized that God is One to be feared and understood that God has all authority. It is the same way that we might approach a person of accomplished status. For us, it could be a professional athlete, a business owner who has done fantastic things, or a dignitary in the government. We all consider the way in which we would approach the people that fill these roles. Do we actually consider the position of the Almighty God? Do we consider the Creator of the world, the One who has all power and authority? Do we consider Him, like the tax collector did, as someone to approach with reverence and humility? We walk through this in our initial understanding of the Gospel, our salvation. Do we continue to walk through this in the way we pray, give, fast, and worship God? Is our giving based on our humility and obedience to God? Is our approach to prayer based on our own agenda? Can we say not my will but Thine be done? When we fast, are we looking at it as a way to lose weight, a fad, or a diet? Can we see it as an expression of our humility towards God and worship Him in the way we approach Him?

Jesus used the example of the one who is full of pride in contrast to the one who walks in humility. The statement of the tax collector versus the statement of the religious Pharisee is insanely contrasting.

- The words of the Pharisee: *"God, I thank you that I am not like other men, extortioners, unjust, adulterers, or even like this tax collector. I fast twice a week; I give tithes of all that I get."*

- The words of the tax collector: *"God, be merciful to me, a sinner!"*

Take a moment and examine your own life. Have you ever compared yourself with other people? Did this make you feel superior to others? Did this make you degrade yourself? I was reading through John chapter 17 as I was writing this, and I came to the part where Jesus prays for His disciples and He prays for us, the future disciples. There is an incredible verse in there that makes this element of worship even better. We are not humbling ourselves to a God who has His thumb on us. We are humbling ourselves to a God who, in a mighty way, expressed His love to us. As Jesus walked through His desire for the disciples and for us, He says in John 17:23, *"I in them and you in me, that they may become perfectly one, so that the world may know that you sent me and loved them even as you loved me."*

Look at that last part of the verse. The reason God sends His disciples out into the world is so that the world will know that God loves them equal to and in the same way that the Father loves the Son. John 17:26 says, *"I made known to them your name, and I will continue to make it known, that the love with which you have loved me may be in them, and I in them."*

Humility is an important part of our worship to God. As we have been examining this study on fasting, the word humility may not be the first thing you thought of or even compared fasting to. My hope is that as you work through the different passages in Scripture, you will see the element of humble worship that takes place in fasting. We need to be examining our motive, heart, and desire by which we engage in fasting and ensure that we follow the example laid out for us in the person of Jesus.

HYPOCRITICAL AND AUTHENTIC FASTING

DEVOTION #6 - PASTOR JOHN CARTER

If we go back and review some of the primary ideas associated with fasting in Scripture, we start to really see how the element of humility directly correlates with it.

Fasting has an expression of mourning.
Fasting has an expression of repentance.
Fasting has an expression of seeking God.
Fasting has an expression of seeking God's protection.
Fasting has an expression of loving your neighbor.
Fasting has an expression of prayer.

Every single aspect of fasting points to a relationship and dependence on God. As one mourns and weeps for loss or pain, they need to rely on the person of God to sustain them through that time of grief. When we walk through repentance and forgiveness, we need to rely on the cross and the person of Jesus to cleanse us from all of our iniquity. When we are lost and have no idea what direction we should be walking, we need to go to God and trust the guidance the Holy Spirit gives us. When we are afraid and anxious, we need to depend on the power and grace of God to get us through those scary moments. When we engage in walking after the things God desires for us, we need to be clear on how we are to love our neighbors. When we talk to God and have those intimate conversations that are just between Him and us, we need to remember who is God and who He is not. The whole element is designed to help us know God. Fasting is a good thing. I would encourage you to try it. Do it with the leading of the Holy Spirit in you. Seek direction, protection, forgiveness, comfort, love, and relationship in the process of drawing close to your amazing Lord and Savior. I am certain that God will show up in ways you cannot even fathom when we authentically walk through fasting the way Jesus laid it out for us. The Father, Son, and Holy Spirit make life personal. They desire a very close and intimate relationship with you and they want you to draw near to them. Fasting is one of the ways we can participate in worshiping the Father, Son, and Holy Spirit. The warning of Matthew chapter 6 is to ensure that it is in fact genuine and authentic.

Matthew 6:16-18 says, *"And when you fast, do not look gloomy like the hypocrites, for they disfigure their faces that their fasting may be seen by others. Truly, I say to you, they have received their reward. But when you fast, anoint your head and wash your face, that your fasting may not be seen by others but by your Father who is in secret. And your Father who sees in secret will reward you."*

The comparison between one who is a hypocrite versus one who is genuine and authentic in their fasting is pretty straightforward in Jesus' own words. Today, rest in this aspect of fasting; it is an element that God has set up. It is a way for us to express our humility to God. It requires our dependence on Him. It shows that we value closeness with Him over anything else, even the feeding of our bellies. It reminds me of James 4:7-10, *"Submit yourselves therefore to God. Resist the devil, and he will flee from you. Draw near to God, and he will draw near to you. Cleanse your hands, you sinners, and purify your hearts, you double-minded. Be wretched and mourn and weep. Let your laughter be turned to mourning and your joy to gloom. Humble yourselves before the Lord, and he will exalt you."*

Jesus desires our humble hearts to draw near Him. He wants it to be real and not just something you do for the show and for boasting. If you have not examined this passage, please spend some time reading this example Jesus Himself gave us. I am only going to give you the response Jesus gives to the devil when He is tempted in the flesh. Pay close attention to the words of Jesus. He teaches us some really important things that have to be at the forefront of our worship of the Father.

- *"Then Jesus was led up by the Spirit into the wilderness to be tempted by the devil. And after fasting forty days and forty nights, he was hungry. And the tempter came and said to him, 'If you are the Son of God, command these stones to become loaves of bread.' But he answered, 'It is written, 'Man shall not live by bread alone, but by every word that comes from the mouth of God.'"* Matthew 4:1-4

- *"Jesus said to him, 'Again it is written, 'You shall not put the Lord your God to the test.'"* Matthew 4:7

- *"Then Jesus said to him, 'Be gone, Satan! For it is written, 'You shall worship the Lord your God and him only shall you serve." Then the devil left him, and behold, angels came and were ministering to him."* Matthew 4:10-11

Jesus' use of God's Word to resist temptation is very powerful. We see Jesus affirming the Scriptures as one of the most important elements of our worship of Him. It is not just passively reading the Scripture, but intimately knowing it and how it applies. He also establishes this element of not testing God the Father. As we engage in fasting, the devil knows how to attack our flesh and its weakness. Jesus shows us that we rule over our flesh through the power of the Spirit. The promise that He resides in us should be a very real and powerful encouragement. Lastly, Jesus expresses the importance of ensuring that our worship is solely devoted to the Father and nothing else. Our service to Him must be singularly focused and not allow other things to distract us from that. Today, take some time to focus your worship on God the Father, Son, and Holy Spirit.

LESSON EIGHT

Laying Up
Treasures in Heaven

PASTOR CHUCK LINDSEY

"Do not lay up for yourselves treasures on earth, where moth and rust destroy and where thieves break in and steal; but lay up for yourselves treasures in heaven, where neither moth nor rust destroys and where thieves do not break in and steal. For where your treasure is, there your heart will be also." Matthew 6:19-21 (NKJV)

1. What are some examples of earthly treasures?

_____

_____

_____

2. What are some examples of heavenly treasures?

_____

_____

_____

"Have money, but never let it have you" is a phrase I have heard often through the years. As an adult, I understand the warning. The pursuit of money and possessions is a trap. It promises to give, but actually takes everything to gain it and then holds the person who chases it. This is what is conveyed in Paul's words to young pastor Timothy in 1 Timothy 6:9-10 (NKJV), *"But those who desire to be rich shall fall into temptation and a snare, and into many foolish and harmful lusts which drown men in destruction and perdition. For the love of money is a root of all kinds of evil, for which some having strayed from the faith in their greediness, and pierced themselves through with many sorrows."* As His people, we chase what is better. We look not for temporal (earthly) rewards. We intentionally lay down that pursuit and seek His eternal reward.

3. Is money evil? Is it wrong to have a savings account?

_____

_____

_____

With this in view, Jesus says in verse 19, *"do not lay up"* *"treasures"* here. *"Lay up"* comes from the Greek verb "thesaurizo" and means "to gather or to store up for safe keeping."

The definition of this word reveals the absurdity of the task! It is laughable. Even the most careful and meticulous "storing up" does not ensure safekeeping! We cannot really keep any "thing" long-term. Every "thing" has a clock. The mountains of electronic trash in other parts of the world are full of what was, at one time, the must-have new gadget. Peter reminds us that *"all these things will be dissolved"* (2 Peter 3:11, NKJV). Our world is filled with the remnants of things that were once desired and are now discarded. It all dissolves.

4. Can you think of something that you felt you had to have that disappointed?

_____

_____

_____

In the same way, alarms, locks, cameras, chains, covers, and safes, are all designed to protect what we have from being taken. We spend nearly as much to protect what we have as the thing itself. Though the Pharaohs of Egypt were all buried with their treasure, not one carried it beyond the tomb. Most were simply robbed after the fact! It is these two truths about "things" that Jesus warns about when He says, *"Moth and rust destroy and where thieves break in and steal."* *"Destroy"* comes from the Greek word "aphanízō" and means "to corrupt, spoil, or take away." The lesson here is that earthly goods can be easily lost and have to be continually protected!

In contrast to this, Jesus tells us that there are reliable investments in life. They are investments that are sure and cannot lose value (look at your 401k!) and will not be taken from us! He says, *"but"* which means "instead." We are to *"lay up for yourselves treasures in heaven."* How is this possible? How do we store up and gather treasures for Heaven? The answer is found in everything we have already looked at. When we do what we do for His reward instead of the reward of men, we are storing up eternal rewards. When we serve or give, seeking only His approval and to be seen by Him rather than others, we are investing in something that is sure. He assures us that *"neither moth and rust **destroy** and where thieves **break in** and **steal**."* Again, Peter reminds us of these better investments when he writes that we have *"an inheritance incorruptible and undefiled and that does not fade away, [as is] reserved in heaven for you"* (1 Peter 1:4, NKJV). The contrast between these "treasures" could not be stronger. One we cannot hold onto as it continually slips through our hands. The other can never be taken from us!

5. Incorruptible, undefiled, and does not fade away sounds great. What is the worst warranty experience you have had?

_____

_____

_____

In verse 21, Jesus peels back the veneer of desire and asks the question that is behind it, "What do you want?" Verse 21 forces us to examine what we really want for both time and eternity. Jesus masterfully probes, *"For where your treasure is, there your heart will be also."* His words make us look inside, to ask, "What exactly is my treasure?" His words are simple to understand. The *"**treasure**"* is what I see as valuable. The *"**heart**"* expresses my affection and attention. If my treasure is my money, my mind is on it all the time. If my treasure is my car, I will park it as far away from others as possible! If my treasure is my position, my importance, or my influence, my focus will center around those things. If however, my treasure is my family, my effort and attention will prove this. If my treasure is my King, my Savior, and Lord, my life will demonstrate that. It is all too easy to see what people *"**treasure**"* because their *"**heart**"* (affections, attention, and words) follow it. For some it is a sports team, for others, it is the stock market, and someone else it might be a hobby. People talk about what they are into. As in young love, we gush over what we are in love with. If He is my treasure, my life, affections, and attention will confirm it!

6. Is it wrong to have nice things or to take care of them? What is the balance?

_____

_____

_____

Matthew 6:22-23 continues, *"The lamp of the body is the eye. If therefore your eye is good, your whole body will be full of light. But if your eye is bad, your whole body will be full of darkness. If therefore the light that is in you is darkness, how great is that darkness!"*

From the heart, we turn now to the eyes. Jesus warns that we must be careful with what we take into the *"body"* through the *"eyes."* While this short section applies to many areas of life, Jesus is still talking about loving money. This is seen in verse 24, *"You cannot serve [both] God and mammon." "Serve"* comes from the Greek verb "douleúō" and means "to serve and carry out the will of another."

"Mammon" was the (false) "god" of riches and wealth. So again, while this section has application to many areas of life, Jesus is still talking about the way that riches can capture both our attention (eyes) and affections (heart)!

7. How does marketing attack our eyes?

_____

_____

_____

He gives us a picture and says, *"The lamp of the body is the eye."* In that day, a *"lamp"* was a small clay vessel that held oil, had a small wick, and a handle for carrying. Its primary (and obvious) purpose was to help a person see in darkness. Its glow-in-the-dark revealed where to go and what to avoid. Jesus says that our eyes are like these *"lamps,"* but rather than shining out, they shine into our bodies. Therefore, He says, *"If therefore your eye is good,"* which seems to mean that our light is shining and unhindered by sin and evil. It means that what is being taken in by the eyes is good and right. He says, if *"your eye is good, your whole body will be full of light."* In simple terms, this means that what we take in affects us. If we take in the good, we are affected in a good way. Light is shone through the body. However, the warning in verse 23 is that the opposite is also true. The words *"but if your eye is bad"* means that sin is affecting the light. Sin and evil being taken in through the eye are snuffing out the light or covering it in some way. The result, Jesus says, is that our *"whole body will be full of darkness."* It is a warning that means we are always affected by what is taken in through our eyes. To not have light is to walk in darkness. To walk in darkness is to not know where to go or what to do. It means that we will not know what to avoid and will eventually trip and fall. Jesus puts an exclamation point on this by saying, *"If therefore the light that is in you is darkness, how great is that darkness!"* This means that if the only thing being taken in is wickedness, the result is tremendous spiritual blindness and severe consequences in life.

8. How should this affect what we watch on our TV, cable, computer, and phone?

_____

_____

_____

While this can and does refer to anything we might take into our body through our eyes, both good and bad, it primarily refers to the *"treasure"* that He has already spoken of. If riches and wealth are our *"treasure,"* it captures both our attention (eyes) and our affections (heart). However, if the Lord is our *"treasure"* and if His reward is what we seek, then He has both our attention (eyes) and affection (heart). Verse 24 makes it clear that a choice must be made because *"no one can serve two masters."*

9. How are some ways we can give God our attention (eyes) and our affections (heart)?

_____

_____

_____

Matthew 6:24 says, *"No one can serve two masters; for either he will hate the one and love the other, or else he will be loyal to the one and despise the other. You cannot serve God and mammon."*

When you stop to consider the words *"no one can serve two masters"* you realize immediately that this is obviously true. *"Serve"* comes from the Greek verb "douleúō" and means "to serve and carry out the will of another"

10. Have you ever had two bosses? How did it go?

_____

_____

_____

I once worked at a company where I had two bosses who hated each other! Their hatred of each other created something of a chess match where each was trying to outdo the other or catch the other in some error. Unfortunately, we common employees were just pawns in their game. When one of them heard the direction given by the other, they would overrule that and give an order that was directly opposite. It was maddening! It is this scenario that Jesus describes with the words *"no one can serve two masters."* The word *"serve"* also carries the idea of "belonging to or being subject to another" and it reveals a truth that any unsaved person does not want to hear. We are all owned by someone. We are not our own. We never have been! The idea that we are our "own man" is patently false and a lie designed to keep us in a false sense of independence from God. The truth is, we did not make ourselves and therefore we ultimately belong to the One who made us. However, the Bible says that through sin we can enslave ourselves to a new master and this is what has happened! Mankind through sin enslaved himself to the god of this world, the devil, to do his evil bidding. It is only through repentance (turning from sin) and turning to God that we become slaves of a new Master. It is giving ourselves to Him (Romans 6:16).

Satan is a cruel master. Jesus said (John 10:10, NKJV)) that *"the thief"* only wants *"to steal, and to kill, and to destroy."* In contrast, Jesus as our Master is loving, gentle, and kind. In the same passage, Jesus contrasted Himself with *"<u>the thief</u>"* and said, *"I have come that they may have life, and that they may have it more abundantly."* The New Testament makes it clear that there are only two *"masters"* and we are all owned by one or the other. As Christians, we are happily owned by the One we call Master and Lord, our King Jesus. The unsaved person is also owned, often unaware, by the god of this world who hates them and laugh's at their demise. Jesus' words make it clear that we cannot have two masters. It is one or the other. We cannot serve two masters. It is one way or the other.

11. Do you think most unsaved people would understand that we all have a master?

_____

_____

_____

He says, *"For either he will <u>hate</u> the one and <u>love</u> the other."* *"<u>Hate</u>"* comes from the Greek verb "miseo" and means "to detest." *"<u>Love</u>"* comes from the Greek verb "agapao" and means "to love dearly, tenderly."

Both words express deep emotion towards whichever master we have. It is painful to know that people *"<u>hate</u>"* (detest) my Master, the King, and Victor over all, the Lord Jesus whom I *"<u>love</u>."* However, I understand it, for I *"<u>hate</u>"* (despise, detest) their master, *"that serpent of old"* (Revelation 12:9, NKJV) who has forever lost and is the devil whom they *"<u>love</u>."* Jesus said a person will be *"<u>loyal</u> to the one and <u>despise</u> the other."* *"<u>Loyal</u>"* comes from the Greek word "antechomai" and means "to hold firmly to." ***"Despise"*** comes from the Greek word "kataphroneo" and means "to look down on with contempt!"

We come back to the words ***"you cannot <u>serve</u> God and mammon"*** and again make the point that either God is Master and "calls the shots" or money does. There is no in-between.

NOTES

HOW TO PREPARE
DEVOTION #1 - PASTOR JOHN CARTER

"Do not lay up for yourselves treasures on earth, where moth and rust destroy and where thieves break in and steal, but lay up for yourselves treasures in heaven, where neither moth nor rust destroys and where thieves do not break in and steal. For where your treasure is, there your heart will be also. 'The eye is the lamp of the body. So, if your eye is healthy, your whole body will be full of light, but if your eye is bad, your whole body will be full of darkness. If then the light in you is darkness, how great is the darkness! No one can serve two masters, for either he will hate the one and love the other, or he will be devoted to the one and despise the other. You cannot serve God and money.'" Matthew 6:19-24

We are steadily moving through Matthew Chapter 6. This week we are going to walk between this great chasm of earthly treasures versus heavenly treasures. We will examine our earthly vision versus heavenly vision, and determine if we serve earthly masters versus the Heavenly Master. So, the question is, "How do you prepare for this massive disruption in how we think, see, and serve?" It is easy to ignore and it is easy to create very real reasons why we cannot focus our minds. Consider what we see and ultimately commit to serving a wonderful God.

I am sure you have a million other things on your mind as you are preparing for the week. Your mind is more than likely not really into even reading this devotion. I get it! You are not going to offend me one little bite if you say, "I am too busy for this." If you can endure the business of life and squeeze in a little time to finish the devotions this week, I hope you will be challenged and encouraged as you learn to focus your heart, mind, and soul towards God. By doing this, we will have greater peace and understanding of the important things of God.

In the business of life, how do we prepare for God's disruption? Jesus set an example of this element of disruption for us quite often as He walked the Earth. It seems Jesus was often interrupted during His mission to complete the work His Father had sent Him to do. In Luke chapter 5, we see a story of Jesus' teaching being interrupted by a group of men trying to get one of their friends before Jesus so He could heal him.

Luke 5:18-19 records, *"And behold, some men were bringing on a bed a man who was paralyzed, and they were seeking to bring him in and lay him before Jesus, but finding no way to bring him in, because of the crowd, they went up on the roof and let him down with his bed through the tiles into the midst before Jesus."*

Can you imagine how disruptive this would have been? Jesus is trying to teach all these people (the crowds) when these guys have the audacity to interrupt Him. They literally tear open the roof and deconstruct a home so that they can get access to the One who can heal. Consider the massive interruption that took place in this scene!

I would think Jesus would be so upset by the interruption and that they destroyed this home. I This is often my own response to disruptions in my life. We find them inconvenient, annoying, and sometimes just outright angering. Look at the example Jesus gave us during His own disruption. Luke 5:20 says, *"And when he saw their faith, he said, 'Man, your sins are forgiven you.'"*

The disruption that was initially caused by these men who cared for their friend turned into an even bigger one with the statement Jesus just made, *"Your sins are forgiven you."* What did He say? The people that heard Jesus say this instantly were disrupted by the words of Jesus, in particular the so-called religious people. Luke 5:21-22 says, *"And the scribes and the Pharisees began to question, saying, 'Who is this who speaks blasphemies? Who can forgive sins but God alone?' When Jesus perceived their thoughts, he answered them, 'Why do you question in your hearts?'"*

I love how Jesus likes to disrupt our thinking and He knows how to get us to disrupt the routine and patterns we create in our hearts. He knows all the questions we are going to walk through and He knows the real and tangible ways we are going to be disrupted. Be willing and ready for it! In Luke 5:23-26, we see Jesus doing something amazing, *"'Which is easier, to say, 'Your sins are forgiven you,' or to say, 'Rise and walk?' But that you may know that the Son of Man has authority on earth to forgive sins' - he said to the man who was paralyzed - 'I say to you, rise, pick up your bed and go home.' And immediately he rose up before them and picked up what he had been lying on and went home, glorifying God. And amazement seized them all, and they glorified God and were filled with awe, saying, 'We have seen extraordinary things today.'"*

Disruptions can definitely be hard to deal with. We have our plans and our agendas. We think we know what we want and when something else comes in and throws it off, we can easily take it the wrong way. I see Jesus, in this story, taking the disruption and using it to glorify God. He uses it to point us to His power and His authority. Jesus took the disruptions and turned them into glory, awe-filled wonder, and made them extraordinary. So, how do I prepare for the disruption of God? I think it starts with the willingness to be disrupted. If we are too busy for God to interrupt our day, then we can easily say our priorities are off. This week, as we look at Matthew 6:19-24, ask God to disrupt your days, thoughts, and priorities so that we can experience the glory, wonder, awe, and extraordinary things God has prepared for us.

This week's study will more than likely be disruptive. It will cause you to question things in your own life. This disruption is not a bad thing. As much as we may feel uncomfortable, the goal is to draw us closer to the Father. The desire of God in His disruptions is to help us see the things we need to see so we can be even more aware of how He desires to be with us. Today, take some time and pray that God will disrupt your life (Yes, I said pray for it). Pray that the disruption will point out some things you need to address. Pray that the disruptions will ultimately cause you to draw near to Him, the One who has all authority and power to forgive sins! He has the healing power to fix what is broken in us! When He does this, let us make sure we praise His name and give Him glory for every single disruption we encounter.

RESULTS OF EARTHLY TREASURES
DEVOTION #2 - PASTOR JOHN CARTER

"Do not lay up for yourselves treasures on earth, where moth and rust destroy and where thieves break in and steal." Matthew 6:19

Yesterday, we talked about the disruptions of God. Get ready to be disrupted, church. We are going to hit some of the very real and uncomfortable things we, as the American Church, have fallen prey to. We do not like this kind of disruption. If I am being honest, this is a very uncomfortable devotion to write for me. I do not like talking about this subject. I would rather not discuss it. God does not let me just hide and not deal with things that need to be dealt with. I hope as we walk through these next few days, you will know my heart. It is not my desire to "punch you in the face." It is to bring to light what Jesus is teaching. In that process, it may feel like a "punch." I am feeling it, too.

The initial statement Jesus makes in this teaching is this idea of treasures, specifically *"treasures on earth."* Another way to say it might be earthly treasures. What are your earthly treasures? Can you take just a few seconds and determine what you would consider to be your treasure? I love how Jesus helps us identify what our treasures might be. What do you fear losing the most? What are you most afraid of being stolen or destroyed? This identification process can often help us point to what we treasure.

I remember doing a construction project for a man back when I used to swing a hammer. He was a very wealthy man. He lived in a very large house with a very large barn out in front. My work was predominately at the house so I never ventured to the barn. One day I asked him, "Why is your barn so big? What do you keep in there?" I was absolutely blown away by his response. He started to tell me it was where he would keep his cars and airplanes. He said he had another warehouse full of cars and planes in another city. The fact that he had planes and cars was not the part that blew me away. He proceeded to tell me how he had the building completely secured both in environmental and theft prevention aspects. He then made the following statement, "Not even God can get my cars and planes wet." I share this story not to make you disparage this man, but to help you see a man who treasured earthly things. What are the things you treasure? What are the things that you claim as your own? What are the things in your life that, "Not even God can get to?" Maybe a nicer way of saying it would be, what are some things in your life that God cannot disrupt? These things are often the things we treasure and value the most.

Paul teaches a young pastor some incredible things in the book of 1 Timothy. One of those things has to do with riches, wealth, and money. In 1 Timothy 6:8-10, he writes, *"But if we have food and clothing, with these we will be content. But those who desire to be rich fall into temptation, into a snare, into many senseless and harmful desires that plunge people into ruin and destruction. For the love of money is a root of all kinds of evils. It is through this craving that some have wandered away from the faith and pierced themselves with many pangs."*

Here, we see Paul expounding on the earthly treasures. He establishes that those who desire to be rich (desire earthly treasures) will fall into a temptation, that is, *"a snare."* It is senseless and harmful. It will lead to ruin and destruction. This love for wealth, money, or earthly treasure is at the root of all kinds of evil done by those who desire it. He even goes on to explain that it is the source of wandering away from the faith, or nearness of God. The result is that by the pursuit of this desire, the craving leads to many pangs. Pangs are intense anxiety, anguish, grief, and pain. This is the outcome of focusing on earthly treasures.

If you think through all of this, you can understand why this is the result that follows when we value earthly things. All earthly treasures have an expiration date. They rust even if they are put in perfect environments. They can be stolen or damaged. Have you ever been to someone's house that was super protective of all their trinkets that are laid out all over the home for others to see? It can be funny to see the stress they go through trying to protect their items, especially if you brought kids with you. They want to have a good time and fellowship with you, but their mind is so overwhelmed by the need to protect their treasures they cannot rest or enjoy the company that is in front of them. Often times, this is another way we can identify what our treasure is - we want to show it off to other people.

Do you feel disrupted yet? I know I do! I do not want to leave it here as my goal is not to destroy but to build up. Continue reading 1 Timothy and you will see the amazing work of Jesus. In 1 Timothy 6:13-16, there is praise and honor that is bestowed upon Jesus by Paul, *"I charge you in the presence of God, who gives life to all things, and of Christ Jesus, who in his testimony before Pontius Pilate made the good confession, to keep the commandment unstained and free from reproach until the appearing of our Lord Jesus Christ, which he will display at the proper time - he who is the blessed and only Sovereign, the King of kings and Lord of lords, who alone has immortality, who dwells in unapproachable light, whom no one has ever seen or can see. To him be honor and eternal dominion. Amen."*

Paul then continues his discussion on how the rich are to respond with their riches. In 1 Timothy 6:17-19, Paul shows how not to hold onto these earthly treasures, *"As for the rich in this present age, charge them not to be haughty, nor to set their hopes on the uncertainty of riches, but on God, who richly provides us with everything to enjoy. They are to do good, to be rich in good works, to be generous and ready to share, thus storing up treasure for themselves as a good foundation for the future, so that they may take hold of that which is truly life."*

Here we are introduced to the pitfalls of those who trust in their riches rather than trusting in God. When the reliance on our earthly treasures takes over, we tend to get arrogant and prideful. We think that our treasures are what our hope is in. We trust in the security of wealth instead of the security of God. If you are a big *"Lord of the Rings"* watcher, I imagine you can envision the character, Gollum, as he hangs on to his "precious."

Paul does not just stop with the warnings, but he leans into the things the rich are to do with the wealth God has allowed them to have. They are to do good with it. They are to be generous and **"to be rich in good works."** Paul continues by laying down some serious heavenly financial planning. He talks about laying down a good foundation for the future by storing up treasures for Heaven. Tomorrow, we will walk through heavenly treasures. Paul is saying the same thing Jesus did in Matthew chapter 6, there are two ways to go about the things we call treasure. One way results in leading to trouble, evil, harm, and serious difficulties. The other leads to that which is truly life. I would like to choose the latter over the first.

Today, let God disrupt your earthly treasures. Lean on Him to point them out and really work through in your heart what you are holding onto. God wants to show you a way that leads to an incredible life.

HEAVENLY TREASURES
DEVOTION #3 - PASTOR JOHN CARTER

"But lay up for yourselves treasures in heaven, where neither moth nor rust destroys and where thieves do not break in and steal. For where your treasure is, there your heart will be also."
Matthew 6:20-21

Yesterday, we walked through earthly treasures. Today, we are going to examine a clear "do versus do not" scenario. In other words, do not do this (laying up treasures on earth); however, definitely do this other thing (laying up treasures in Heaven). We are going to examine what it looks like to pursue heavenly treasures, which ultimately reveals the true place of our hearts. Be prepared to be disrupted through this process. You may see some things revealed that may hurt or feel uncomfortable. When we go through those things, it is called refinement (aka: sanctification).

Let us look through some passages that will lay a solid foundation for what heavenly treasure is and what it looks like.

- *"Lift up your eyes to the heavens, and look at the earth beneath; for the heavens vanish like smoke, the earth will wear out like a garment, and they who dwell in it will die in like manner; but my salvation will be forever, and my righteousness will never be dismayed."* Isaiah 51:6

- *"Listen to me, you who know righteousness, the people in whose heart is my law; fear not the reproach of man, nor be dismayed at their revilings. For the moth will eat them up like a garment, and the worm will eat them like wool, but my righteousness will be forever, and my salvation to all generations."* Isaiah 51:7-8

Starting off, we see the Kingdom of Heaven including the concepts of eternity and righteousness. We also see the elements of this physical earth and sky have an end date. It is like a garment that will wear out and be no more. The sky will dissipate as smoke does. However, in complete contrast to the sin-riddled Earth, the spiritual, eternal Kingdom of Heaven will remain forever. The righteousness of God is written to be forever. Salvation, which is a free gift for us to receive, is also something that will be forever. It is important to really wrap our minds around this idea of temporary versus eternal because it is the foundation of where we decide to keep our treasures. Jesus tells us another story in Matthew 19:16-22, **"And behold, a man came up to him, saying, 'Teacher, what good deed must I do to have eternal life?' And he said to him, 'Why do you ask me about what is good? There is only one who is good. If you would enter life, keep the commandments.' He said to him, 'Which ones?' And Jesus said, 'You shall not murder, You shall not commit adultery, You shall not steal, You shall not bear false witness, Honor your father and mother, and, You shall love your neighbor as yourself.' The young man said to him, 'All these I have kept. What do I still lack?' Jesus said to him, 'If you would be perfect, go, sell what you possess and give to the poor, and you will have treasure in heaven; and come, follow me.' When the young man heard this he went away sorrowful, for he had great possessions."**

That is not what a lot of rich and wealthy people want to read. We see the eternal presented with the man's request. Clearly, there is an element of eternality that we all have scripted in our hearts. I love, just like in Isaiah, Jesus teaches that if you want to understand what is good (or righteous) go read it in God's Word. Jesus quotes half of the Ten Commandments. The point is that Jesus Himself says that if you want to know what the Father considers good (or righteous) you can start there. It is interesting that this young man further pursues something he feels he is lacking. If he is able to live out the righteous commandments of God, how is it that he, in his own questioning, felt something lacking? He asks, **"What do I still lack?"** then Jesus instructs him to do two things.

First, He tells him to sell all of his earthly possessions and give them to those in need. This is a very prominent teaching in Scripture, caring for the needy and the poor. The righteous rulers made provision for this and every time they did these things, they were commended. Jesus also links this act of caring and providing for the poor as a means to store up treasures in Heaven.

Second, He says to this man, *"Follow me."* As I examine this story, we see this man deny both of the instructions Jesus gave him. He did not follow Jesus because it is recorded that he *"went away,"* which is the opposite of *"follow me."* It also records for us the condition of the man's heart; he went away full of sorrow. If you look back at yesterday's study you will recall that sorrow is one of the results of seeking earthly possessions. We get a clear picture of the condition of this wealthy man's heart. He clearly had a huge amount of trust and faith in his earthly possessions. So much so, that when Jesus challenged him to give it all up, he could not do it. I am not suggesting that you go out and live on the streets, but we do need to examine if we, like that man, have put our trust and faith in our own personal wealth. If we lost it all, would we still trust God? Would we still praise Him? In Luke 12:32-34, we read, *"Fear not, little flock, for it is your Father's good pleasure to give you the kingdom. Sell your possessions, and give to the needy. Provide yourselves with moneybags that do not grow old, with a treasure in the heavens that does not fail, where no thief approaches and no moth destroys. For where your treasure is, there will your heart be also."*

In both the Matthew and Luke accounts, we see Jesus attributing the heavenly treasures directly to caring and providing for the needy and the poor. James 5:1-6 adds, *"Come now, you rich, weep and howl for the miseries that are coming upon you. Your riches have rotted and your garments are moth-eaten. Your gold and silver have corroded, and their corrosion will be evidence against you and will eat your flesh like fire. You have laid up treasure in the last days. Behold, the wages of the laborers who mowed your fields, which you kept back by fraud, are crying out against you, and the cries of the harvesters have reached the ears of the Lord of hosts. You have lived on the earth in luxury and in self-indulgence. You have fattened your hearts in a day of slaughter. You have condemned and murdered the righteous person. He does not resist you."*

James follows the same principles laid out by Paul in the letters to Timothy, that treasures of the world will bring misery and sorrow. In verse 6, we see James link the murder and condemnation of Jesus Christ to the rich person that puts their faith and trust in their wealth over their trust and faith in the person of Jesus. In other words, if you continue to rely on the treasures of this world over the eternal treasure of Heaven (Jesus), you will bear the guilt of His murder and condemnation. That is a serious warning.

Peter teaches us a similar aspect of the heavenly treasures in 1 Peter 1:3-5, *"Blessed be the God and Father of our Lord Jesus Christ! According to his great mercy, he has caused us to be born again to a living hope through the resurrection of Jesus Christ from the dead, to an inheritance that is imperishable, undefiled, and unfading, kept in heaven for you, who by God's power are being guarded through faith for a salvation ready to be revealed in the last time."*

Peter points to this amazing salvation we have in Christ; however, he also speaks of this incredible inheritance that is being held for us in Heaven. It is an inheritance that is imperishable, undefiled, and unfading. What is this inheritance? What is this treasure? It is the Kingdom of Heaven! It is where we receive the eternal, glorified, resurrected body that is just like Christ's resurrected body. It is our salvation, our hope of dwelling in the presence of God and being with Jesus. It is a treasure that is greater than silver and gold! It is more valuable than anything we could imagine.

Romans 8:12-17 adds, *"So then, brothers, we are debtors, not to the flesh, to live according to the flesh. For if you live according to the flesh you will die, but if by the Spirit you put to death the deeds of the body, you will live. For all who are led by the Spirit of God are sons of God. For you did not receive the spirit of slavery to fall back into fear, but you have received the Spirit of adoption as sons, by whom we cry, 'Abba! Father!' The Spirit himself bears witness with our spirit that we are children of God, and if children, then heirs - heirs of God and fellow heirs with Christ, provided we suffer with him in order that we may also be glorified with him."*

This is very disruptive to our modern culture because our world teaches us to go after all the earthly treasures. Our measure of success is often determined by how much earthly treasure we possess. We have been dupped into the temporary and have lost sight of the eternal. The church is not immune to the influence of the current culture. We choose to lift up the things that have little eternal value and ignore the call to go after the heavenly treasures. Our focus needs to be on the lives and souls of the lost, needy, poor, and destitute. We can emphasize the glories of this fading earth and ignore the eternal state of those around us. Do we value our possessions and our wealth above the needs and souls of those around us? The choice is ours.

These passages are often very difficult for a wealthy nation like America to read and hear. We find this kind of thinking to be very disruptive and uncomfortable. I trust the Holy Spirit to reveal in you the specific issues related to earthly, temporary things you have elevated. I pray that the disruption God produces in each and every one of us will lead us to rely more on Him and elevate the eternal things He has gifted to us to distribute. I pray we will learn the righteous things to pursue and partake in the eternal Kingdom of Heaven.

As both Matthew and Luke conclude this matter, they ultimately point us to the condition of our hearts. **"Where your treasure is, there will your heart be also!"** Does your heart belong to Jesus? Does it desire Him? Does it value the person and treasure of a relationship with Jesus? Is your heart fixed on the eternal things of

God? Is it pursuing the mission of the Kingdom? This is the ultimate question that disrupts all other disruptions. When we get real and truly focus on our actions, our priorities and the condition of our heart becomes so clear. Pray that God will mold your heart to conform to His image, character, and desires. The goal is that we would start to think according to a heavenly economy (eternal) versus an earthly economy (temporal).

EARTHLY VISION

DEVOTION #4 - PASTOR JOHN CARTER

"The eye is the lamp of the body. So, if your eye is healthy, your whole body will be full of light, but if your eye is bad, your whole body will be full of darkness. If then the light in you is darkness, how great is the darkness!" Matthew 6:22-23

As Jesus continues to disrupt our comfortable, temporary state of mind when it comes to our finances, He seems to shift the subject to the way we see things. Ironically, they are both related. Yesterday, we walked through the eternal versus the temporary. Jesus is going to address a very similar aspect of life only in a different metaphor, light versus darkness. Maybe a better way to say it is what we allow to be seen through our eyes. Jesus starts off by making a very direct and factual statement. *"The eye is the lamp of the body."* Yesterday, we were seriously disrupted by the way our hearts clearly miss priorities by choosing temporary things over eternal things. Jesus is continuing His teaching on the heart. It is the motive, if you will, of how we view others in this world. It is how we view sin and how we view God. This whole week, Jesus is challenging our view on finances and how oftentimes we allow the temporary comfort of money to lead us away from the things of God. We allow it to lead us into sin.

Jesus is teaching us to examine the way we see things. This is not a new concept in Scripture. In Deuteronomy 15:7-9, Moses writes, *"If among you, one of your brothers should become poor, in any of your towns within your land that the Lord your God is giving you, you shall not harden your heart or shut your hand against your poor brother, but you shall open your hand to him and lend him sufficient for his need, whatever it may be. Take care lest there be an unworthy thought in your heart and you say, 'The seventh year, the year of release is near,' and your eye look grudgingly on your poor brother, and you give him nothing, and he cry to the Lord against you, and you be guilty of sin."*

This passage in Deuteronomy fits perfectly with what Jesus is teaching in Matthew chapter 6. You see it mentioned twice as the aspect of the heart. He says, not to *"harden your heart"* against the poor and needy." He then adds, do not have *"an unworthy thought in your heart"* against your poor or needy brother. This is fitting for the previous three days of devotions. Now, I want to focus on the part that talks about the eye, *"Your eye look[s] grudgingly on your poor brother."* This is talking about the way we allow our hearts to be influenced by the way we look at or see others. If you know someone will not be required to repay you, do not choose to look down on that person and refuse to offer the finances to help them with their needs. This is a sin according to the Bible. In 1 John 3:16-18, we see it said another way, *"By this we know love, that he laid down his life for us, and we ought to lay down our lives for the brothers. But if anyone has the world's goods and sees his brother in need, yet closes his heart against him, how does God's love abide in him? Little children, let us not love in word or talk but in deed and in truth."*

John is teaching us to mimic the behavior of Jesus and the Father. They are One. The challenge today is to not let only what we can see be the determining factor in how we help others. We have already talked about the reliance on money for our own security, now we are challenged to examine how we can help others in the family of God. John, like Deuteronomy, is challenging us to not close our hearts against our fellow brothers or sister in Christ. John actually takes it a step further. Just like Jesus gave His life for us, John tells us to be willing to give our life for our fellow brothers and sisters in Christ. Do you feel uncomfortable yet? John goes the extra mile to say that we are not doing this with just our words or talk, but with our actions. This can feel very uncomfortable.

Ephesians 4:17-19 says, *"Now this I say and testify in the Lord, that you must no longer walk as the Gentiles do, in the futility of their minds. They are darkened in their understanding, alienated from the life of God because of the ignorance that is in them, due to their hardness of heart. They have become callous and have given themselves up to sensuality, greedy to practice every kind of impurity."*

The biblical message to not walk in darkness (sin) is pretty evident. We see over and over again the connection to all of this is our heart. This is a serious message that we, the church, need to examine on all levels. Do we make temporary things more important than eternal things? Are we allowing the darkness of sin to cloud our vision of the heavenly things?

Jesus, in Matthew chapter 6, continues to show us the sin that we allow to cloud our vision, *"But if your eye is bad, your whole body will be full of darkness. If then the light in you is darkness, how great is the darkness!"* The sin of partiality and greed is mentioned in James. It is actually talked about throughout all of Scripture. It is what Jesus is trying to teach us regarding how we treat the brothers and sisters that are less fortunate. It is how we sin against the Creator of humanity. We allow our earthly vision to take over and make sinful judgments against other brothers and sisters in Christ. Paul talks about this darkness in Acts 26:15-18, *"And I said, 'Who are you, Lord?' And the Lord said, 'I am Jesus whom you are persecuting. But rise and stand upon your feet, for I have appeared to you for this purpose, to appoint you as a servant and witness to the things in which you have seen me and to those in which I will appear to you, delivering you from your people and from the Gentiles - to whom I am sending you to open their eyes, so that they may turn from darkness to light and from the power of Satan to God, that they may receive forgiveness of sins and a place among those who are sanctified by faith in me.'"*

We see in Paul's story, Jesus Himself expounds on the teaching in Matthew chapter 6. The darkness is sin. How great is that darkness in you? Recognizing that our earthly vision is clouded by sinfulness is important to understand as we allow Jesus to disrupt our earthly vision. In Acts, we see Jesus expounding on the power of God to turn us from darkness to light. We can receive the heavenly treasure of forgiveness and the sanctification that comes through faith in Jesus. We need to be willing to allow the Light of Heaven (Jesus) to open our eyes to start seeing things with heavenly eyes versus earthly eyes. It is to see things with a healthy eye that lets the full light in.

Today, consider if you need to approach someone you have made harsh judgments against. It could be for whatever reason. Maybe they dress differently than you, look different than you, or are poorer than you. Do not let a day go by where you are allowing your vision to be clouded with the darkness of the world and sin. Jesus may be opening your eyes to an area in your life you have not allowed the light of Heaven to shine on. Maybe it is greed or the desire and pursuit of money. Maybe you have neglected your family (children) and justified it with financial aspects and gains. Ask God to open your eyes to see with full 20/20 vision the things He has called you to change. Correct the unhealthy eye and be moved to see with the full light. I am going to go deal with my own disruption that God is causing. Be blessed!

WHO IS YOUR MASTER?
DEVOTION #5 - PASTOR JOHN CARTER

"No one can serve two masters, for either he will hate the one and love the other, or he will be devoted to the one and despise the other. You cannot serve God and money." Matthew 6:24

All this week Jesus has been challenging our earthly thinking in comparison to the way He desires us to think. He recognizes the condition of our hearts and how we have a very strong propensity to lean on our shallow, earthly view of life. He has been challenging me to stop thinking in this temporary way and expand my views to see things from a heavenly perspective, an eternal one. We have walked through many hard-to-hear things regarding the way we view money or wealth. Jesus takes it to a whole new level at the end of the passage we are looking at this week. Jesus asks us to whom our heart is devoted. Yes, this still has to do with money and wealth. I think Jesus knows that we as humans tend to put a lot of trust in our earthly possessions.

If I can be completely transparent with you, this subject has been a hard one for me. I am not sure if you could sense my struggle in the writing. Emotion is often hard for me to put down in written form. If you do not know my story, I went to school for finance. I dreamed of becoming a "successful" businessman and obviously having plenty of money in the bank account was at the core of my motivation. God had a different plan for my life. As often as I tried to resist it, He called me into ministry. One of the most amazing things I have ever had the privilege of walking through, was when God called me and my family to South Carolina. I went through a refining process that was like none other I had ever been through before.

God put me in a position where I was no longer the primary financial provider of the home. I was the stay-at-home dad. Covid really solidified this role for me as I was instantly responsible for the education of three daughters. There was a season when I was very bitter against God. I was very confused about what He was doing why He was doing it. I really started struggling through where I was in life. I considered my college education from a top state university had way more value to it than how I was using it. When I got my degree, I was a workaholic. I would work a full-time job and do school at night to pursue my ambitions. Often times, I would be gone from 5:30 am to 9:30 pm. I did all this with a family. Trusting my wife to do all the heavy lifting of raising a family, I went after the earthly things. I share this with you because I think it very much applies to the hard, disruptive topic we are walking through. As I found myself in a completely different role than I had ever imagined (stay-at-home dad), I found myself walking more in the things of the earth than I had realized. God was tearing down the things I put security in. God had to disrupt my life to show me where my heart was. I look back at the many lessons I learned during that time and often find myself full of joy. I find myself with joy because now I see that the disruption was very needed in my life. I needed God to snap me out of my earthly view of things and put me focused on the heavenly things that He has called me to.

In verse 24, Jesus lays it out as clear as day concerning the condition of our hearts. He illustrates it in terms of masters. "Boss" might be a better and more current word to use. He says that you cannot have two bosses (masters). Jesus points out that just like in real life, it is difficult to try to please two completely different people. Maybe you have two completely different bosses where one likes things done a certain way and another likes it done in a completely different way. The inner turmoil of that scenario is a very real one if you have ever been in that situation. What ends up happening is you end up choosing one over the other. It is usually the one you like more. Jesus then flips this example to tell us the way we serve money and the way we serve God are very much just like this example of two bosses. It is two bosses that are completely different. One, an earthly boss, sees and desires you to do things one way. He wants you to store earthly treasures and have an eye for earthly things. The other, the Heavenly Boss, has a completely different way of doing things. He wants you to lay up your treasure in a place that is eternal. He desires you to see things in this life with a heavenly mindset. Ultimately, we have to choose which one we will serve. All too often, we are deceived by the pursuit of money and wealth. We fail to see the misery and sorrow that comes with it and can even destroy our families all for the pursuit of money. We can easily justify our motives for the love of money. We put words in there like, "I am doing this for my family. I am going to make all the money I need then serve God." We, as the church, easily walk through this as well. We will justify the way we spend money to bring glory to an organization or up our church comfort experience. Yet, in the same breath, we are ignoring the people we can help sitting right next to us.

So, the ultimate question is, who is your master? Who have you chosen to devote your time, energy, and resources to? Which one do you really despise? No doubt, these are seriously hard and disruptive questions to try and navigate through. I really do understand the hardship of these questions. I write them and cringe because I know my own heart. I know how for many years I have relied on, and still have the propensity to rely on, my own financial stability. It is a dangerous trap the devil sets for us. In James 4:4, it is said this way, ***"You adulterous people! Do you not know that friendship with the world is enmity with God? Therefore whoever wishes to be a friend of the world makes himself an enemy of God."***

I do not want to be an enemy of God, nor do I want to make money a master of my life! Being forced to walk through our heart condition when it comes to money is truly disruptive. It is completely and totally opposite of the way the world tells us to view it. The world tells us money is the answer. They say, "Cash is king." I cannot count the number of times I have heard those very words in negotiating a deal.

Cash is not king; Jesus is King! Take some time today and truly work through the disruption. Is there something you are holding on to way too tight? Do you see an area in your life that if God tries to navigate you towards, you are quick to pull it away and say, "Not that, God. You cannot touch that." Please, do not take another day to allow your heart to be convinced of the lies that wealth, money, or the pursuit of money, puts before you. Choose today to serve God and follow Him!

PROMISES OF GOD
DEVOTION #6 - PASTOR JOHN CARTER

Praise Jesus! It is Saturday. That means today is the completion of this very difficult topic. As we conclude this week's devotions, hopefully we have been able to identify some areas God needed to disrupt in our lives. I want to lay out some tangible ways to rest in the promises of God. A lot of the subject this week was directed specifically to the rich or the wealthy. It was directed to those who may be putting a lot of their hope and faith in their bank account. I want to give you some Scriptures to read today that will help if you are anxious about what it feels like to be without. Maybe all this week you are sitting there saying, "It is easy to say all these things if you are not buried in bills." You might be thinking that money matters! You cannot live without it. One of the first steps I had to walk through in my own life, was dealing with anxiety. I often quickly go to Hebrews 13:5-6, *"Keep your life free from love of money, and be content with what you have, for he has said, 'I will never leave you nor forsake you.' So we can confidently say, 'The Lord is my helper; I will not fear; what can man do to me?'"*

I really had a hard time with the part about being content. I never considered myself as one who loved money, but man, I sure did struggle with the part about being content. The promise in this passage is that God will never leave or forsake us. Make it personal. Put your own name in this promise. "God will never leave John Carter nor will He (God) forsake John Carter." Sometimes we need to hear it out loud. We allow doubt, fear, and anxiety to take over. The next part of the verse is just as powerful. Through my needs, God allows me to walk through difficult things so that I can only give glory to Him. I cannot claim my own victory. I do not get to say look at how well I figured it out. That is all worldly, selfish, prideful, and the desire to glory in my own abilities. The later part of the verse says, "John Carter gets to claim God as his helper! John Carter does not need to fear!" Wow! Hold on to that promise. You can put your name in there where it says to not fear, not to be anxious, and not to doubt God's ability to care for you.

Paul gives a very similar encouragement in Philippians 4:11-13, *"Not that I am speaking of being in need, for I have learned in whatever situation I am to be content. I know how to be brought low, and I know how to abound. In any and every circumstance, I have learned the secret of facing plenty and hunger, abundance and need. I can do all things through him who strengthens me."*

Paul walks us through understanding what it means to be content. The *"secret"* is knowing who to rely on. It does not matter if you are reading this in your abundance or in your need. Paul says that the strength of God is what carries him through. Later on, in Philippians 4:19-20, he says, *"And my God will supply every need of yours according to his riches in glory in Christ Jesus. To our God and Father be glory forever and ever. Amen."*

Maybe the abundant place you find yourself is exactly how God wants to provide for someone who is hungry and in need. This is the challenge for the week. Are we willing to disrupt our lives and comfort to be used by God in a way that glorifies Him?

Another promise passage I go to is Psalm 37. It is honestly one of my favorite passages. I am pretty good at masking my internal doubt and anxiety. If you know me, you may not even consider me to be one who struggles with this in my life. I do, however, for reasons I will not venture into today, struggle with doubt, fear, and anxiety. I remind myself often by reading God's Words for me. The first 8 verses of Psalm 37 are encapsulated with the struggle of fretting, *"Fret not yourself because of evildoers; be not envious of wrongdoers! For they will soon fade like the grass and wither like the green herb. Trust in the Lord, and do good; dwell in the land and befriend faithfulness. Delight yourself in the Lord, and he will give you the desires of your heart. Commit your way to the Lord; trust in him, and he will act. He will bring forth your righteousness as the light, and your justice as the noonday. Be still before the Lord and wait patiently for him; fret not yourself over the one who prospers in his way, over the man who carries out evil devices! Refrain from anger, and forsake wrath! Fret not yourself; it tends only to evil."*

Often times our worry, stress, doubt, and fear come from not looking at what David says to look at in this Psalm. The answer is in the midst of the struggle.

- *"Trust in the Lord."*
- *"Delight yourself in the Lord."*
- *"Commit your way to the Lord."*
- *"Be still before the Lord."*
- *"Wait patiently for him [the Lord]."*

Later on, in Psalm 37:25-26, David adds, *"I have been young, and now am old, yet I have not seen the righteous forsaken or his children begging for bread. He is ever lending generously, and his children become a blessing."* Psalm 37:39-40 continues, *"The salvation of the righteous is from the Lord; he is their stronghold in the time of trouble. The Lord helps them and delivers them; he delivers them from the wicked and saves them, because they take refuge in him."*

The whole Psalm is a very encouraging promise to grasp. This week, I hope and pray your world was disrupted. I hope you will be taught by God to take refuge in Him over the temporary things of this world. Rest in the promises of God knowing that He sees your needs and He cares for you. In my life, I have witnessed many times how God showed up when I needed Him the most! When all I could do is say, "The Lord is my Helper!" I cannot wait to see you all at our Gathering! We need each other to carry on through some of the more difficult times. We need to remind each other how much God cares for each and every one of us.

Matthew 6:19-24 says, *"Do not lay up for yourselves treasures on earth, where moth and rust destroy and where thieves break in and steal, but lay up for yourselves treasures in heaven, where neither moth nor rust destroys and where thieves do not break in and steal. For where your treasure is, there your heart will be also. The eye is the lamp of the body. So, if your eye is healthy, your whole body will be full of light, but if your eye is bad, your whole body will be full of darkness. If then the light in you is darkness, how great is the darkness! No one can serve two masters, for either he will hate the one and love the other, or he will be devoted to the one and despise the other. You cannot serve God and money."*

LESSON NINE

Do Not
Be Anxious

PASTOR CHUCK LINDSEY

"Therefore I say to you, do not worry about your life, what you will eat or what you will drink; nor about your body, what you will put on. Is not life more than food and the body more than clothing? Look at the birds of the air, for they neither sow nor reap nor gather into barns; yet your heavenly Father feeds them. Are you not of more value than they? Which of you by worrying can add one cubit to his stature? So why do you worry about clothing? Consider the lilies of the field, how they grow: they neither toil nor spin; and yet I say to you that even Solomon in all his glory was not arrayed like one of these. Now if God so clothes the grass of the field, which today is, and tomorrow is thrown into the oven, will He not much more clothe you, O you of little faith? Therefore do not worry, saying, 'What shall we eat?' or 'What shall we drink?' or 'What shall we wear?' For after all these things the Gentiles seek. For your heavenly Father knows that you need all these things. But seek first the kingdom of God and His righteousness, and all these things shall be added to you. Therefore do not worry about tomorrow, for tomorrow will worry about its own things. Sufficient for the day is its own trouble." Matthew 6:25-34 (NKJV)

Someone at this point might say, "Well, I do not think that money is my "master" or "god," but I do worry about it! I need it! I do not always know what is going to happen." To this Jesus says what He says in verse 25.

1. How can I know if money is too important in my life?

_____

_____

_____

"I say to you" is our Lord's way of saying to us, "Hear Me, hear now what I am saying to you about providing for yourself in this life." This immediately presents us with a choice. It is a choice between what "we" or the "world" says about these things and what God says about them. What God says is always true! He cannot lie. He cannot be wrong. So what He says here, about providing for ourselves, is

true in every circumstance, for all people, throughout all of human history.

2. What is the theme of this section?

_____

_____

_____

Jesus hits the nail on the head with the words, *"Do not worry about your life."*

"Worry" comes from the Greek word "merimnáō" and means "anxious, troubled in mind or thought."

Our society seems to be continually plagued by anxiety. We hear the word used in various contexts all the time. Anxiety, fear, worry, and stress are all describing different aspects of the same thing: uncertainty. These are the by-products of being unsure and uncertain in life. This uncertainty is the very issue Jesus is addressing! He wants us as His people, to be sure of something. He wants us to know for certain that something is true. He wants us to be sure of Him. He wants us to be certain that He loves us. He wants us to be sure that He cares and that He is the One who provides. He wants this certainty to extend into every category of life and free us from the fear, stress, and worry that uncertainty always brings.

3. How do worrying and having control issues relate to each other?

_____

_____

_____

He begins by telling us that we do not need to worry about our lives. That is a striking thing to say! According to our Lord, there is no need to ever fear or be troubled or anxious in life. Wow. Some of us might have just laughed at the thought of never worrying. However, this is actually possible for His people and Jesus tells us how.

He begins by giving common examples of areas we are tempted to stress about. *"What you will eat or what you will drink"* is the fear that will we not have enough to eat and that we and our families could starve. This is not something we need to fear or worry about. He tells us this in verse 26 with the words, *"Look at the birds of the air, for they neither sow nor reap nor gather into barns; yet your heavenly Father feeds them. Are you not of more value than they?"*

"Value" comes from the Greek word "diaphérō" and means "to carry something (as precious or valuable)."

4. What comes to mind when you think of the word *"value"*?

_____

_____

_____

Notice how Jesus tries to quell this fear of starving? He tells us to be sure of Him and His love for us. He does not, for instance, say, "Do not worry about what you will eat, because there is plenty of food and there is a good chance you will find something to eat!" No! He says, "I am taking care of everything, and especially you." He wants you and me to be sure of how much He loves us. *"Are you not of more value than they?"* is meant to quiet our fears, calm us, and bring us to a place of trust and thankfulness. In short, He wants me to be certain that I do not have to worry because He provides and loves me!

5. Summarize this last paragraph in your own words.

_____

_____

_____

The words in verse 25 (*"nor about your body, what you will put on"*) summarize more than just a worry about having necessary clothing. It is any physical need we might have. To this, He says in verses 28-29, *"So why do you worry about clothing [or house payments or the gas bill]? Consider the lilies of the field, how they grow: they neither toil nor spin; and yet I say to you that even Solomon in all his glory was not arrayed like one of these."* Then, to quench our worry, He says in 30, *"Now if God so clothes the grass of the field, which today is, and tomorrow is thrown into the oven, will He not much more clothe you, O you of little faith [little certainty, little assurance]?"* We see the same pattern in these words as before. If He is taking care of and providing for what is insignificant, how much more will He provide for us? The lesson is simple. We do not need to worry or stress about our needs because He is the provider and actually does love us supremely.

6. What are some common things people worry about?

_____

_____

_____

It is interesting when you really stop to think about worry, fear, anxiety, and stress. For all the energy these things take, they do not give anything in return; not anything good that is! These things do not change the outcome of anything! Worrying about illness does not change whether you get sick or not. Stressing about losing your job, does not prevent job loss. Fear of dying does not keep us alive longer. Countless studies have shown what we already know: these human responses are destructive and take a tremendous toll on us as people. This is the point that Jesus is making in verse 27 when He says, *"Which of you by worrying can add one cubit to his stature?"*

7. What are some negative outcomes of worrying?

_____

_____

_____

"Worrying" comes from the Greek verb "merimnáō" and means "to be apprehensive, have anxiety, be (unduly) concerned, troubled."

It has been said, "Worry does not empty tomorrow of its sorrow. It empties today of its strength." It is so true! I am not accomplishing anything at all as I fret and stress and worry about what might happen. This is something that I personally need to be reminded of often. There are many things that I simply do not worry about. The fear of something suddenly happening to my wife or children is a constant battle for me. I have spent many nights needlessly worrying about my sick children's breathing! As I read these words from Jesus, I know that my worrying did not keep their airways open. He did. He does. My worrying about a car accident taking my wife from me does not put a protective bubble around her as she drives. I wish it did! He is her protector. He loves her. He loves me. He loves my children. He is in actual control and He is good. Here, Jesus is telling us to quit it! Our worrying is not preventing or helping anything!

8. Where are some areas of worry you need to turn over to God?

_____

_____

_____

Therefore, He says in verses 31-32, *"Therefore do not worry, saying, 'What shall we eat?' or 'What shall we drink?' or 'What shall we wear?' For after all these things the Gentiles seek."* He is reminding us that these are the concerns of those who do not have God as their Father. These are the worries of those who have no one watching over them, looking after them, and providing for them. These are the fears of those that do not know Him. It is painful to see that I have acted like someone who does not know Him when I have worried about the things we need. I have acted as though I do not have Him, Who is limitless in His power, resources, and care as my Father. Lord, please forgive me! The end of verse 32 is meant to reset us. Each word is important and builds as one brick upon another to form the secure home we should live in, *"For your heavenly Father knows that you need all these things."*

9. How does one become a child of God?

_____

_____

_____

"__Knows__" comes from the Greek verb "oída" and means "to see and know completely."

What a thing for God to convey to us! What promises He wants us to be sure of! First, He is my *"Father."* This means that I am His child and He wants me to see our relationship this way. He is a true and good Father caring for me, His child. Next, He is our *"heavenly Father"* which of course tells us that He is also God, but speaks to His limitless resources to provide. Then we are told that as a good Father, He both sees and *"__knows__"* what we need. Amazing! God pays attention to me. That is the thing He wants us to be sure of. He knows. He sees. He cares.

As we come into verse 33, we have to back up to verse 25 for a moment. It is there that Jesus asks a question that is a needed reminder to us all. He asks, *"Is not life more than food and the body more than clothing?"* This question is meant to make us pause and reflect on the meaning and purpose of life. Life is more than the temporal things I am worried about. We all know that it is more than what we eat, what we drink, or the clothes we have. Real life is much deeper than these things. Life is more than just making it through or surviving each day. A meaningful life is full of meaningful things. At the top of this is relationships. Boiled down, life is about two main things:

> 1. To know God (relationship with Him).
> 2. To make Him known (relationship with others).

The wealthiest people in the world who have "everything" are among the most miserable because life is about more than things. Jesus said this in Luke 12:15 (NKJV), *"Take heed and beware of covetousness [a desire for more than is never satisfied], for one's life does not consist in the abundance of the things he possesses."* How true this is! Jesus makes this clear with His question, "Isn't life about more than these things?" In other words, "It takes a lot of energy to worry about these things and they are not even things you need to worry about."

He continues this thought in verse 33 when He tells us, *"Seek first the kingdom of God and His righteousness, and all these things shall be added to you."*

"Seek" comes from the Greek verb "zētéō" and means "to seek after, look for, strive to find."

10. What comes to mind when you think of the word *"seek"?*

_____

_____

_____

The word *"seek"* is a word that describes our goals, priorities, focus, effort, and attention. Verse 33 makes us ask, "What am I trying to find? What am I trying to accomplish? What am I doing with my life?" It is a serious question. The word *"first"* forces us to evaluate the order our priorities are in. What do I *"seek"* above all other things? If we are honest we might say, "I seek my personal comfort or happiness" or "I seek above all other things making more money or a higher position at work." These pursuits might not be wrong in the right place, but they are certainly wrong at the top!

Jesus tells us to *"seek first the kingdom of God."* What does this mean? It means that above all other pursuits in life that we might have, our lives are to be about accomplishing His will. Simply, it is to try to do what He is wanting rather than what we are wanting. This applies to all categories of life. I need to pursue what He wants in my marriage, in my parenting, in my work, in my neighborhood, and in my hobbies. As His people, we ask, "What do you want Lord?"

The goal is to bring about His *"kingdom"* in our lives. Simply put, His *"kingdom"* is anywhere where He is King. His *"kingdom"* can be brought into our marriage when He is King and we are doing what He wants us to do in our marriages with our spouses. His *"kingdom"* is brought about in our parenting when He is King and we are carrying out His will and direction in our parenting. His *"kingdom"* can be brought into our workplace as we serve Him and follow His direction and lead in every aspect of our work life. To *"<u>seek</u> first the kingdom of God"* is to put Him first and His will at the top of our priorities. When we do this, everything else falls into its proper order.

11. Are there any areas of your life you now need to turn over to God and let Him rule over them?

_____

_____

_____

Our design as human beings is at the root of this command from Jesus. We have been designed by Him to seek Him first and His will first. That is how we have been designed to live. It is how we work best. To say it another way, we do not do well as people with anything else in the first place of life's pursuits. Many examples can be given, but consider the man or woman who makes their career the first priority and pursuit of life. Many other things, important things, and meaningful things are sacrificed for this empty pursuit. Make money the thing you *"<u>seek</u> first"* and watch all of life's meaning and purpose drain from your life. Even seeking *"first"* good things, such as a good marriage, being a great parent, or being a productive member of society (whatever that means), will result in frustration because the order is wrong. We have been designed to seek God first. This is the only *"first"* pursuit that does not sacrifice everything else to do it. What I mean is, every other *"first"* pursuit sacrifices everything else to accomplish it. However, to *"<u>seek</u>"* Him first and His will, we find that we still have the capacity to pour into every other area of our lives the way that we ought to. This is because the order is correct and this is our design.

An illustration here is, I think, helpful. As a teenager, I learned that every vehicle's engine has a specific timing order. The timing order is the order in which the spark plugs fire; which in turn, forces the pistons down. This is what propels the car forward. I learned about this when this order was out of whack in one of my first cars. I remember trying to drive it. It was stuttering, stopping, and the engine would die suddenly. It was loud, things were popping, and needless to say, it did not get me down the road at all. That is when I learned that the order of those spark plugs and pistons firing was extremely important. It has been an illustration to me ever since. When the timing is wrong, the car does not go anywhere. When the order is wrong in life, the "car" does not go anywhere. Jesus' command is simple, put Me and what I want at the top, and if you do, everything else will lock into place.

That is the promise in the remainder of verse 33, *"But seek first the kingdom of God and His righteousness, and [if we do] all these [other] things shall be added to you."* Again, the promise here is that if we put Him and what He wants at the top, everything else will fall into place. This is not a promise that life will become easy and free from all difficulty. It is a promise that life will make sense, have real meaning, and we will have all we need to do all that He has called us to do. This is an extremely liberating promise from our Lord!

12. What does seeking God first mean in your life?

_____

_____

_____

Lastly, we read the words in verse 34, *"Therefore do not worry about tomorrow, for tomorrow will worry about its own things."* This is a fitting conclusion for everything Jesus has just said to us. The word *"therefore"* is a word that points us back to everything He has just said. In other words, "Because I am your Father, because I love you, because I know your need, and because I am infinitely capable of providing for you; *'therefore do not worry.'"*

"**_Worry_**" comes from the Greek word "merimnáō" and means to be "anxious, troubled."

What is going to happen? What is next? What will tomorrow bring? We do not know. However, we know Who does! It has been said, "We do not know what the future holds, but we know who holds the future." This is a basic but important truth. We must remind ourselves often. No man can predict what will happen. The future is God's domain and His alone. We do not need to **_"worry"_** about tomorrow because of everything He has already said. He is in control, loves us, and watches over us. We have already said it, but worrying about tomorrow does not empty tomorrow of its trouble; it only empties today of its strength. We are not stopping anything or changing anything by our worry. It is a fruitless, exhausting exercise that takes a heavy toll on us as people. To this Jesus says to let tomorrow **_"worry about its own things. Sufficient for the day is its own trouble."_**

13. Write out some of your worries in the form of praise or thankfulness to God.

_____

_____

_____

Jesus' words in this chapter are meant to cause His sheep to simply trust Him as the Great Shepherd. When you and I are tempted to panic, we must quickly remind ourselves of these truths and come back to a place of trust and rest in who He is and what He has said. We really do not need to worry because we are His and He loves us.

NOTES

PROMISES OVER FEAR AND ANXIETY

DEVOTION #1 - PASTOR JOHN CARTER

This week we are going to walk through the very real element of anxiety. This seems like an appropriate path to follow as Jesus just showed us some of our very real and often deceiving areas that we tend to cling to for security. Last week, Jesus walked us through earthly treasures versus heavenly treasures. He walked us through how to see things from a heavenly perspective versus seeing things from an earthly perspective. The truth is that walking through that can often lead us to a place of anxiety or fear. I love how Jesus is so aware of our human condition that He immediately talks to us about where our heads go next. A lot of our worrying can start with the phrase, "What if?" It can be things like, "What if I cannot feed my family, lose my house, or do not have clothes to wear?"

This week we are going to walk through these very real and important "what if" concerns through the eyes of Jesus, which is a heavenly perspective. The main passage we will be breaking down is Matthew 6:25-34. Each day, we will take a portion of this passage and look at other Scripture to help us understand the meaning and application for our lives.

Matthew 6:25-34 says, ***"Therefore I tell you, do not be anxious about your life, what you will eat or what you will drink, nor about your body, what you will put on. Is not life more than food, and the body more than clothing? Look at the birds of the air: they neither sow nor reap nor gather into barns, and yet your heavenly Father feeds them. Are you not of more value than they? And which of you by being anxious can add a single hour to his span of life? And why are you anxious about clothing? Consider the lilies of the field, how they grow: they neither toil nor spin, yet I tell you, even Solomon in all his glory was not arrayed like one of these. But if God so clothes the grass of the field, which today is alive and tomorrow is thrown into the*** *oven, will he not much more clothe you, O you of little faith? Therefore do not be anxious, saying, 'What shall we eat?' or 'What shall we drink?' or 'What shall we wear?' For the Gentiles seek after all these things, and your heavenly Father knows that you need them all. But seek first the kingdom of God and his righteousness, and all these things will be added to you. 'Therefore do not be anxious about tomorrow, for tomorrow will be anxious for itself. Sufficient for the day is its own trouble.'"*

What is the initial thought that comes to your mind as you read that passage? Is it comfort? Is it a passage that internally makes you feel good? Do you tend to see the pessimistic part or do you see the promise?

When I read this text, I tend to see all the areas that are problematic. My mind shifts to the parts that can raise some questions. It is the parts that, in my head, I question, "Can I trust this?" Maybe you are completely different in that regard and you see the promising parts first. Having a little bit of an understanding of the human condition, I would venture to say more of us can relate to the problematic statements than we can to the statements of promise. Let me give you an example of what I am talking about. *"Do not be anxious about your life,"* is completely opposite of my natural thinking. I tend to do everything I can to protect my life and make sure my life does not incur any unnecessary harm. In fact, we are taught as kids to do this very thing: to protect ourselves from any element of danger or discomfort. We teach kids that in order to grow up and be strong, we need to eat healthy foods. I am pretty certain that, as a kid, my parents convinced me that I had to eat the very thing I hated most, peas.

The truth is there is a lot in this passage that has "promise" written all over it. We tend to allow our earthly vision to take over and only see things from our earthly perspective. Are there a few in this passage that make you think? While we will address those through the coming week, I think it is important to examine an element of

Scripture that often gets left unaddressed. That is the worthiness of the Word of God. It deserves our trust.

I find myself having to correct my perspective, especially when I read something that challenges some of my basic natural instincts. I have found that in order to correct my earthly view, I need to remind myself of the trustworthy aspects of God that I already believe in. For example, "Does God love me?" I have no problem believing that. I can show you tons of Scripture that affirm it as well. I can also tell you real stories of how His love was shown to me over and over again. Most believers can, more than likely, do the same thing. Another question could be, "Did Jesus forgive me?" In this series, we have looked at that very subject, the forgiveness of God. Those who have received that forgiveness and the promises of that forgiveness, tend to have very little reserve in accepting it. There may be times when we doubt it, but we often go back to the very Word of God to affirm the original promise we received. Those are just a few examples of things I remind myself of that I know I can trust. So, when I read something that sends me to a part of my head that questions the very statement, I am reminded of the things I know I trust. You may have your own areas of Scripture that you have nailed down and know you can trust. When we hear or see things that cause us to question, we need to examine the "why" in, "Why do I not trust this?"

As I write this I am reminded of Peter's words in 2 Peter 1:12-15, *"Therefore I intend always to remind you of these qualities, though you know them and are established in the truth that you have. I think it right, as long as I am in this body, to stir you up by way of a reminder, since I know that the putting off of my body will be soon, as our Lord Jesus Christ made clear to me. And I will make every effort so that after my departure you may be able at any time to recall these things."* Peter understood the power of reminding ourselves of the truth of God's Word. Jesus Himself, in the high priestly prayer, also pointed us to this very powerful understanding. John 17:17 says, *"Sanctify them in the truth; your word is truth."*

It is part of the human condition to receive elements of truth we like, and seriously question the elements we do not like. Walking through the "why" is incredibly important. Why do I not trust these words but I can trust other words from the same person? I am talking about Jesus, not me. My hope and prayer this week is that God will reveal in your heart some areas of doubt, fear, or anxiety that we can work through. Jesus is not giving us a task that is impossible. He gives us a bunch of promises in these passages. Hopefully, we will learn to trust the promises over the doubt. I pray we will learn to trust the promises over the fear. I hope we will learn to trust the promises over the anxiety. God's words are true and trustworthy. Here are a few verses to encourage you to trust in the words of God.

- *"Trust in the Lord with all your heart, and do not lean on your own understanding. In all your ways acknowledge him, and he will make straight your paths."* Proverbs 3:5-6

- *"The Lord is a stronghold for the oppressed, a stronghold in times of trouble. And those who know your name put their trust in you, for you, O Lord, have not forsaken those who seek you."* Psalm 9:9-10

- *"You keep him in perfect peace whose mind is stayed on you, because he trusts in you. Trust in the Lord forever, for the Lord God is an everlasting rock."* Isaiah 26:3-4

YOU ARE OF MORE VALUE!

DEVOTION #2 - PASTOR JOHN CARTER

Yesterday, we acknowledged that sometimes when we read Scripture, our brains have a tendency to reel back and seriously question what we are reading. We ask ourselves questions, "Can I trust this?" We started to walk down the path of asking the question "why" to doubt, fear, and anxiety directly as it correlated to the trust aspect. We should question, "Why can I not trust this statement?" As we break down these first few verses of Jesus' teaching, keep that thought in your head. Jesus gives us some incredible promises to hold onto that are far more powerful than doubt, fear, and anxiety.

Matthew 6:25-26 says, *"Therefore I tell you, do not be anxious about your life, what you will eat or what you will drink, nor about your body, what you will put on. Is not life more than food, and the body more than clothing? Look at the birds of the air: they neither sow nor reap nor gather into barns, and yet your heavenly Father feeds them. Are you not of more value than they?"*

Jesus gives us two major elements of life that He tells us not to worry about, food and cover. The pessimistic side of me goes off and says, "Easier said than done!" Food and clothing are at the very core of basic necessities. Of all the things in life to consider worrying about, I would think that food and clothing would be okay. It is not like I am worried about who wins the Superbowl. There are a ton of other things Jesus could have put into these passages besides the core of basic human needs. We have so many things in our life to consider and worry about. We have our jobs, finances, car repairs, home repairs, and what our friends think (what they like or do not like on our social media). These are first-world problems. I think this is the very point Jesus is making when it comes to our anxiety and worry. We allow so many things in our lives to consume our thoughts and mind. We tend to worry about things that are actually very minor and insignificant. We tend to make mountains out of molehills.

Jesus is clearly bringing it back to the basics. He is doing it intentionally. Consider the promise Jesus lays out for us. He uses tangible and real things to point us to the heavenly truth. He says, *"Look at the birds of the air."* Consider how they get their food and their basic necessities in life. They do not plant gardens, nor do they have big barns to store food. Yet, the Father feeds them. Here is the part of the promise that you truly have to examine. Jesus asks a rhetorical question, *"Are you not of more value than they?"* The promise is less about the food and more about your worth to God. The promise is about the character of God and how God the Father views you. Take a look at another passage that affirms the very thing Jesus is saying. Psalm 147:8-11 says, *"He covers the heavens with clouds; he prepares rain for the earth; he makes grass grow on the hills. He gives to the beasts their food, and to the young ravens that cry. His delight is not in the strength of the horse, nor his pleasure in the legs of a man, but the Lord takes pleasure in those who fear him, in those who hope in his steadfast love."*

God's promise is that He values us. Pause and think through that very statement. Do you see yourself as a valued child of God? Do you see God as a Father who cares for His children? Just as we walked through the "why" on the pessimistic side, we also need to do the same for the promise side of things. Why do you not see yourself as a valued child of God? Why do you not see God as a caring father? These are the issues at the core of anxiety, fear, and doubt. Where do we put our trust and belief? If we cannot trust God in the basics of human necessity, how can we say we trust Him for anything else? God loves me enough to send His only son, would He then have me starve to death? Hopefully, we can see the disconnect in that thinking. The promise again is in the value God has for us. There are a lot of things in this life that create fear and anxiousness. We often have those fears, doubts, and anxieties because we have lost sight of the promises of God, or we just never believed them to begin with.

"Are you not of more value than they?" It is the ultimate question to address in your life. Is the work of Jesus on the cross something you hold to and believe in? Do you believe the Word of God when it says He did this for you and for me? We can also believe and trust in God when it comes to our nourishment. Jesus brings it back to basics. If there is anything we should be worried about, it is the necessities. Jesus tells us not to even worry about our basic needs. How absurd is it that? We let so many other things that are not even close to the basics consume our minds.

Matthew 10:29-31 adds, *"Are not two sparrows sold for a penny? And not one of them will fall to the ground apart from your Father. But even the hairs of your head are all numbered. Fear not, therefore; you are of more value than many sparrows."* Today, examine your value to God. Are you His child? Does He know you? Do you know Him? John 17:3 says, *"And this is eternal life, that they know you, the only true God, and Jesus Christ whom you have sent."*

Once you have confidently answered the first question, the second question is, "Do you trust His Word?" I do not know exactly what it is that is causing you to fear, doubt, or be anxious. I do not want to dismiss the struggle, because it is real. I want to encourage you to look at the promise over the fear. You are incredibly valuable to God. He cares for you and knows your struggles and difficulties. He wants you to know that He is not far away, but is very near and present. In 1 Peter 5:6-7, we read, *"Humble yourselves, therefore, under the mighty hand of God so that at the proper time he may exalt you, casting all your anxieties on him, because he cares for you."* Trust in the promises of God! Trust that He values you. Trust that He cares for you.

PROMISES

DEVOTION #3 - PASTOR JOHN CARTER

For the last couple of days, we have been examining the double-sided approach to pessimism and promise. Jesus brought it down to the very basic human need for food and clothing. Yesterday, we learned about His promise of value for us. We are going to continue the examination of Jesus' words regarding basic human necessities.

Matthew 6:27-30 says, *"And which of you by being anxious can add a single hour to his span of life? And why are you anxious about clothing? Consider the lilies of the field, how they grow: they neither toil nor spin, yet I tell you, even Solomon in all his glory was not arrayed like one of these. But if God so clothes the grass of the field, which today is alive and tomorrow is thrown into the oven, will he not much more clothe you, O you of little faith?"*

Death is a scary thing to consider! I would think that being anxious about death seems reasonable. Yet, Jesus has a completely different approach. He asks a rhetorical question, "How many of us can actually extend our life by worrying?" I read a survey taken by Milan Dinic of YouGov (from the UK) about being afraid to die. The results stated that 41% were afraid and 43% were not afraid. The remaining 16% were those who said they had not thought about it. In this survey, women (47%) were more likely to fear death than men (35%). The survey points to the fact that this is something we, as humans, contemplate and consider. Honestly, I think it is important to truly consider death and examine your future after death. The reality is, we must all face it at some point. We know because our experience tells us that this body is getting older and weaker. We will eventually die. Hebrews 9:27-28 says, *"And just as it is appointed for man to die once, and after that comes judgment, so Christ, having been offered once to bear the sins of many, will appear a second time, not to deal with sin but to save those who are eagerly waiting for him."*

While the subject of death is not the main focus of today's devotion, take time to consider that question. If you would like someone to reach out to you, text "riverconnect" to 97000. We would love to connect with you.

Now, back to what Jesus is teaching. He says as the book of Hebrews affirms that we are all going to face death at some point. Worrying about it does not change that. Jesus then goes on to talk about another basic fact of life we need: clothing. He compares the lilies of the field to our need of being covered. I am not a botanist, so I probably cannot explain this passage as well as they can; however, I can tell you that a field of lilies is an amazing sight to see. The word Jesus uses, **"glory,"** is a very accurate description of it. Just like the birds of the air, the lilies do not have to work at it to cover the earth. They are not worried about making sure they have the right outfit for the day. They are covered. Next, we see Jesus move to the promise over the fear, anxiety, and doubt.

"Will he not much more clothe you, O you of little faith?" In America, we tend to not worry so much about the covering part as much as we do the brand of the covering. Our anxiety is often rooted more in the ascetics than in the physical. It is highly likely this passage already has a huge disconnect with many of us. We do not really worry if we will have clothes to put on tomorrow. Most of us have closets full of clothing. We do however spend quite a bit of time preparing to be seen by others. I am the father of three daughters. I am also married. We have chosen to have one bathroom in the house. You know where I am going with this thought. My time in the bathroom is very limited with four amazing ladies in my home. The point is, how much time do we worry or stress about how other people view us? Is it something even worth worrying about? I feel that as a father of three daughters, this is an important message to share especially to the ladies reading, you are **"fearfully and wonderfully made"** (Psalm 139:14). The world has created an environment that is super unhealthy, emphasizing body image and how we ought to look and dress. I try to point my girls to the Word of God and tell them and show them how God views them. Just as beautiful as a field of lilies is, how much more are you? In 1 Peter 3:3-4, we read, *"Do not let your adorning be external - the braiding of hair and the putting on of gold jewelry, or the clothing you wear - but let your adorning be the hidden person of the heart with the imperishable beauty of a gentle and quiet spirit, which in God's sight is very precious."*

You are very precious in the sight of God! It is not how you dress or the way you look, but the very character of the person you are. Do not ever forget this promise of God; you are more! You are more than what the world tells you, more than how you feel, and more than your emotions. You are precious in the eyes of God.

I find it interesting that Jesus uses the food and clothing necessities to point us to His amazing promises. Men tend to think with their stomachs and women are often more concerned with how they look. Jesus is pointing us, in either situation, to look at the promises of God. We mean more to God than the most wonderful things on this earth. That is Jesus' promise to us. Do we believe that? Do we hold onto that when we are in the middle of fear, doubt, and anxiety? Jesus concluded the challenge, *"O you of little faith."* Hebrews 11:1 (NKJV) reminds us, *"Now faith is the substance of things hoped for, the evidence of things not seen."*

Faith is not blind (substance) nor is it with proof (evidence). So, when we hear Jesus say, *"O you of little faith,"* I believe He is saying, "Why do you not see the substance and the evidence of who I am?" Take some time today and consider all the blessings God has given to you. Look for the substance of your faith and the evidence of God in your life. Oftentimes, when we only see the pessimistic side, it is because we have not looked for the promising side. I know that God is amazing and there are many things in my life that are truly wonderful and true blessings in my life. I can start by saying that my wife and my kids are an amazing blessing God has given me! My salvation and relationship with Jesus and the Father are a blessing beyond words! It is that easy. Make a list and write them down. When you start to let fear, doubt, and anxiety creep in, you can pull the list out and remember the blessings of God. Trying to wrestle through the difficulties of life and the anxieties that exist in each person's life are a real struggle. We each have our own areas that we need help through. Reach out to a person in the church and ask them to remind you of the promises of God. Let me give you a few promises to meditate on today.

I am saved by grace through faith so all the promises are mine.

- *"That is why it depends on faith, in order that the promise may rest on grace and be guaranteed to all his offspring - not only to the adherent of the law but also to the one who shares the faith of Abraham, who is the father of us all, as it is written, 'I have made you the father of many nations' - in the presence of the God in whom he believed, who gives life to the dead and calls into existence the things that do not exist."* Romans 4:16-17

- *"His divine power has granted to us all things that pertain to life and godliness, through the knowledge of him who called us to his own glory and excellence, by which he has granted to us his precious and very great promises, so that through them you may become partakers of the divine nature, having escaped from the corruption that is in the world because of sinful desire."* 2 Peter 1:3-4

I am created for the great things God has prepared for me.

- *"For by grace you have been saved through faith. And this is not your own doing; it is the gift of God, not a result of works, so that no one may boast. For we are his workmanship, created in Christ Jesus for good works, which God prepared beforehand, that we should walk in them."* Ephesians 2:8-10

I am a new creation. Old things are passed away; all things are made new.

- **"Therefore, if anyone is in Christ, he is a new creation. The old has passed away; behold, the new has come."** 2 Corinthians 5:17

There are so many promises that I could not put them all in this one devotion. Seek out the promises you need to hear. Trust in the Word of God and His promises.

LETTING ANXIETY RULE

DEVOTION #4 - PASTOR JOHN CARTER

"Therefore do not be anxious, saying, 'What shall we eat?' or 'What shall we drink?' or 'What shall we wear?' For the Gentiles seek after all these things, and your heavenly Father knows that you need them all." Matthew 6:31-32

As we walk through the anxieties of this life, we need to hear the words of Jesus. In this verse, He starts off with a strong *"therefore."* James Swanson writes, "The word *'therefore'* is a marker of a result. It means indeed, surely, and then. A marker of a greater emphasis than other markers, but a marker of a relatively weak contrast."

That indicates that what we have learned in previous days, is not in contrast with each other but is closely related. We walked through anxiety and pessimistic viewpoints versus viewing things from the promise. The result is what we previously studied in Matthew chapter 6. The result of the *"therefore"* is closely related to how we understand God's view of us. We see that God views us as valuable and He knows each and every need that we have. He knows we need food, water, and clothing. Since we know that God knows these things, *"therefore"* do not be anxious. If I am to put this bluntly; because we have faith in the promise of who God is, then our anxiety needs to go away. I am reminded of a passage from Paul regarding this verse in Matthew. Philippians 4:5-7 says, *"Let your reasonableness be known to everyone. The Lord is at hand; do not be anxious about anything, but in everything by prayer and supplication with thanksgiving let your requests be made known to God. And the peace of God, which surpasses all understanding, will guard your hearts and your minds in Christ Jesus."*

In previous weeks, we have walked through aspects of prayer. What we heard from Jesus is affirmed again in these two verses. Our *"heavenly Father knows"* what we need and He wants us to pray and make our requests known to Him. He wants our confidence to be in His provision over anything else. I have an amazing 6-year-old daughter. She always goes to her mother when she is hungry. She will go to her and ask for food repeatedly. It is very rare that she comes to me and asks for food. I think she learned that I am not so good in the kitchen and that the provision I give her might not be as good as what Mom would give her. She knows instinctively where the source of the best food comes from. *"Therefore,"* she goes to her mother and asks for the food. I know that might be an extremely oversimplified perspective. However, I believe it is exactly what God is showing us concerning our needs and provisions. We know who the source of our provision and needs comes from, *"therefore,"* we go to the Father and ask. We ask, believe, and trust; that is where the peace of God comes from. It is this very peace on which the promise is given. The promise is that this knowledge will guard (protect) our hearts and minds. Is it not interesting that the two areas of the negative, worry and anxiety, affect the heart and mind? The way to protect us from heart trouble and mind trouble is to go to the source of peace. Just as Paul learned and taught the Philippians to not be anxious and seek the source of peace, we need to learn to do the very same thing.

Peace and anxiety are complete opposites of each other. They are both elements that rule the mind, have impact on the body, and ultimately, point us to the condition of our heart. Were you able to see the promise in Matthew? Did you see the promise in Paul's words? Do they comfort you? Do you still struggle with the details? How is this going to actually work? I find it interesting that Jesus inserts this statement, *"The Gentiles seek after all these things."* I believe Jesus is asking us to really examine where we allow our hearts and minds to go when it comes to provision. When Jesus references the Gentiles, He is simply identifying a group of people that do not have faith or hope in God. Jesus says that even those who have no hope in the person or character of God, seek after this. It is something that is on their mind and affects their motives. In contrast to the Gentiles, we, who know the personal character of

God, should know that our Heavenly Father knows what we need. Do we trust Him to provide? When it comes to this battle between peace and anxiety, we have to examine how we view God.

I rationalize it this way in my own mind; in our society, we call parents that fail to feed, water, or clothe their children as neglectful. In extreme measures, we would even call them abusers for severe neglect. Is God the Father an abuser of His children? Does He neglect His children? When the Bible says that God *"will never leave you nor forsake you,"* do you believe it? He has promised it in His Word.

- *"Keep your life free from love of money, and be content with what you have, for he has said, 'I will never leave you nor forsake you.' So we can confidently say, 'The Lord is my helper; I will not fear; what can man do to me?'"* Hebrews 13:5-6

- *"The steps of a man are established by the Lord, when he delights in his way; though he fall, he shall not be cast headlong, for the Lord upholds his hand. I have been young, and now am old, yet I have not seen the righteous forsaken or his children begging for bread. He is ever lending generously, and his children become a blessing. Turn away from evil and do good; so shall you dwell forever. For the Lord loves justice; he will not forsake his saints. They are preserved forever, but the children of the wicked shall be cut off."* Psalm 37:23-28

As we start to apply the teaching of Jesus to our lives, we see very quickly that His teaching in Matthew chapter 6, is directly related to our understanding of the character of God Himself. If we see God as a person who does not care for His children, is neglectful and uncaring, our heart is going to lean away from the peace and security that God promises to us. Psalm 37 points us to the fact that we are all guilty of tripping up on this trust element of God. However, the reminder is constantly pointing us to the person and character of

God, He will not forsake us. Take today to reflect on your own doubts about the person of God. Really ask yourself if you are showing trust in His character and promises. I find myself often asking this question, "Is it harder for God to save my soul than it is for Him to provide my needs?" When I compare my needs in life to the sins I have committed against God, I can quickly get overwhelmed and appreciate the promise of forgiveness God offers to me. I trust that forgiveness and live with the confidence that the forgiveness offered by God is genuine and real. In 1 John 1:9, we read, *"If we confess our sins, he is faithful and just to forgive us our sins and to cleanse us from all unrighteousness."*

How is it that I can confidently trust in His promise to forgive me of my sins, yet I struggle to trust Him to provide me with my daily needs? If God can save my soul and forgive me of my sins, He most assuredly can provide me with the needs I require to sustain my life. Sometimes, I just need to remind myself of that simple, yet powerful, truth. Be blessed today! Trust in the promises of God in the big things as well as the little things.

LETTING RIGHTEOUSNESS RULE
DEVOTION #5 - PASTOR JOHN CARTER

Matthew 6:33 *"But seek first the kingdom of God and his righteousness, and all these things will be added to you."*

Over the last couple of days, we have examined the negative side of what might consume our thoughts and minds with anxiety, worry, and pessimistic thinking. It is easy to say not to do that and just walk away. In other words, if we focus entirely on the negative thoughts and do not give direction on His promises, then we are not effectively teaching what Jesus says. I love that Jesus says to replace the negative with something that is right and truly positive. Putting this all into context, we see Jesus telling us what not to focus on, and in contrast, to focus on the Kingdom of God and His (God's) righteousness!

This is actually one of the major themes in Jesus' message. As we have examined the Sermon on the Mount, we see that Jesus tells us, all the way back at the beginning of His message (in what is known as the Beatitudes), an interesting thought. Matthew 5:6 says, *"Blessed are those who hunger and thirst for righteousness, for they shall be satisfied."*

Taking what we learned regarding the provision of the Father, it is amazing how the Word of God is linked to helping understand the true priority Jesus is directing us to. Instead of allowing your mind and heart to worry or be anxious about physical food and nourishment, make sure you understand and seek out (hunger and thirst) the Word of God and His righteousness.

What is the righteousness of God? Where do we go to seek it out? Looking back through Jesus' message known as the Sermon on the Mount, we see this theme of righteousness being of significant importance.

- *"Blessed are those who hunger and thirst for righteousness, for they shall be satisfied."* Matthew 5:6

- *"Blessed are those who are persecuted for righteousness' sake, for theirs is the kingdom of heaven."* Matthew 5:10

- *"For I tell you, unless your righteousness exceeds that of the scribes and Pharisees, you will never enter the kingdom of heaven."* Matthew 5:20

- *"Beware of practicing your righteousness before other people in order to be seen by them, for then you will have no reward from your Father who is in heaven."* Matthew 6:1

- *"But seek first the kingdom of God and his righteousness, and all these things will be added to you."* Matthew 6:33

If you just take Jesus' words in the Sermon on the Mount, you will see the following:

1. Righteousness is something that we should desire like we desire food and water.
2. Righteousness is something that we will be persecuted for.
3. Righteousness is something that can exceed that of the religious people.
4. Righteousness is something we should practice, but it should not be flaunted or done for the purpose of others seeing it.
5. Righteousness is something we are to seek after.

In the Gospel of John, we see Jesus also says this regarding the work and purpose of the Holy Spirit. John 16:7-11 says, *"Nevertheless, I tell you the truth: it is to your advantage that I go away, for if I do not go away, the Helper will not come to you. But if I go, I will send him to you. And when he comes, he will convict the world concerning sin and righteousness and judgment: concerning sin, because they do not believe in me; concerning righteousness, because I go to the Father, and you will see* *me no longer; concerning judgment, because the ruler of this* *world is judged."* Jesus says the primary role of the Holy Spirit is to convict those who seek righteousness. He helps define what is right and what is wrong and how to judge correctly. He equates sin with disbelief, unrighteousness toward the Father, and judgment with the devil.

Paul, in the book of Romans, deals with the subject of righteousness. Romans 6:15-19 helps us understand what righteousness is, *"What* *then? Are we to sin because we are not under law but under* *grace? By no means! Do you not know that if you present* *yourselves to anyone as obedient slaves, you are slaves of* *the one whom you obey, either of sin, which leads to death,* *or of obedience, which leads to righteousness? But thanks be* *to God, that you who were once slaves of sin have become* *obedient from the heart to the standard of teaching to which* *you were committed, and, having been set free from sin, have* *become slaves of righteousness. I am speaking in human* *terms, because of your natural limitations. For just as you* *once presented your members as slaves to impurity and to* *lawlessness leading to more lawlessness, so now present your* *members as slaves to righteousness leading to sanctification."* Paul is walking us through the difference between what we say versus what we believe. He uses this metaphor of slavery and creates an incredible contrast to the One we obey. We have a choice to either disobey and be a slave to sin or we can obey and be a slave to righteousness. Paul defines one as lawlessness and the other he defines as righteousness that leads to sanctification. John uses the very same imagery in 1 John 3:4-10, *"Everyone* *who makes a practice of sinning also practices lawlessness;* *sin is lawlessness. You know that he appeared in order to take* *away sins, and in him there is no sin. No one who abides in* *him keeps on sinning; no one who keeps on sinning has either* *seen him or known him. Little children, let no one deceive* *you. Whoever practices righteousness is righteous, as he is* *righteous. Whoever makes a practice of sinning is of the devil, for the devil has been sinning from the beginning. The reason the Son of God appeared was to destroy the works of the devil. No one born of God makes a practice of sinning, for God's seed abides in him; and he cannot keep on sinning, because he has been born of God. By this it is evident who are the children of God, and who are the children of the devil: whoever does not practice righteousness is not of God, nor is the one who does not love his brother."*

Sin is lawlessness! When we go back to Matthew chapter 6, we see Jesus telling us to, *"Seek first the kingdom of God and his righteousness."* As we look at what Jesus is telling us, we start to see that there is a completely contrasting idea of what is right in the eyes of God versus what the devil tries to tell us is right. In fact, from the very beginning in the Garden, the devil has been trying to get us to question the very words and promises of God. When we stop listening to the words of God and start to allow the lies of the devil to creep in, we soon find ourselves walking in contrast to the righteousness of God. This is what we call sin. Paul reminds us of the value of God's Word in 2 Timothy 3:16-17, *"All Scripture is breathed out by God and profitable for teaching, for reproof, for correction, and for training in righteousness, that the man of God may be complete, equipped for every good work."*

Paul points us back to where we learn what righteousness is and that it is rooted in, the very words of the Father and the words of Jesus. In the Gospel of John we see Who it is; that is the Word of God. John 1:1-3 records, *"In the beginning was the Word, and the Word was with God, and the Word was God. He was in the beginning with God. All things were made through him, and without him was not any thing made that was made."* John 1:14 completes the thought, *"And the Word became flesh and dwelt among us, and we have seen his glory, glory as of the only Son from the Father, full of grace and truth."*

"The Word [of God] became flesh." That is talking about Jesus. When we are told to seek first the Kingdom of Heaven and His

righteousness, Jesus is basically saying, "Seek me first! I am the righteousness of God!" If you have bread to eat, water to drink, and clothes to wear, but do not know Him, you have missed it all! Spending time in the God's Word (the Bible) is where we learn how to be trained in righteousness. In other words, it is where we learn to mimic and act out the behavior and character of God and His Son. Take today, and ask yourself, "Am I seeking out the Word of God? Am I seeking Jesus first? Before anything else, I am seeking Him. Be encouraged today that it is not impossible. God gave us the Holy Spirit so that we can confidently know what is right and what is wrong. We have to choose to obey Him and walk in the truth.

THAT'S A WRAP, OR IS IT?

DEVOTION #6 - PASTOR JOHN CARTER

It has been a fantastic journey walking through Matthew chapter 6. We have looked at practicing our righteousness, prayer, and giving in front of other people and what that implies. Going into detail through the Lord's Prayer was awesome! I love how intentional Jesus is in teaching us God's character and how to communicate with Him. Learning about fasting led to dealing with what we trust in, money or God. This week we have been walking through anxiety. There have been many topics we have covered over this series. I trust it has made you think and consider whether you have applied the Scripture correctly to your life. I hope and pray that the challenge of the Bible has deeply impacted you. I pray that you see the words of God as something you can apply directly to your life, today. I find it good to wrestle with the things that are hard and coming to a conclusion on those things is always reassuring. I obviously cannot understand or know how these passages affect you. I know for my life, the timing of writing these devotions and the subject matter is very appropriate. The last passage we have to cover is found in Matthew 6:34, ***"Therefore do not be anxious about tomorrow, for tomorrow will be anxious for itself. Sufficient for the day is its own trouble."***

Hopefully, you are able to take some time this week (or weekend) and enjoy being with your family and lead them in the things of God. This passage is a passage of encouragement, not one that should cause any panic. It is very possible that when you read this text, you here, "There are always going to be things that cause you anxiety, so just deal with the anxiety you have today." I know in my head, I often plan for the worst and hope for the best. It can be a place of much anxiety. This week, I have tried to focus your attention more on the promises than on the pessimistic side of thinking. If you are one who tends to "plan for the worst," you read that verse and cannot help but initiate the worst-case scenario in your mind.

Maybe you are the exact opposite and you are the eternal optimist. I love optimistic people, but find it hard to comprehend how they see everything playing out so perfectly in their mind. My wife is one of these optimistic people and she helps me see that it is not all "worst case" when there is plenty of good and positive things to see, hear, and be joyful over. Just as the passage says, *"Do not be anxious about tomorrow;"* stop and smell the roses. This passage in Matthew reminds me of a passage in James.

James 4:13-17 says, *"Come now, you who say, 'Today or tomorrow we will go into such and such a town and spend a year there and trade and make a profit' - yet you do not know what tomorrow will bring. What is your life? For you are a mist that appears for a little time and then vanishes. Instead you ought to say, 'If the Lord wills, we will live and do this or that.' As it is, you boast in your arrogance. All such boasting is evil. So whoever knows the right thing to do and fails to do it, for him it is sin."* Here, James is addressing the one who may be super optimistic, and planning to make a profit. They are very excited to plan out their future. I see the words of James being completely wise. We do not know what the future holds. We cannot determine the outcome of tomorrow for *"tomorrow will be anxious for itself."* We can think of the best possible outcome or we can think of the worst possible outcome. In both cases, there is the aspect of the will of God. James is teaching us the exact same thing Jesus is teaching in Matthew 6:34. We have today, and what we do with today is what we need to focus our minds on. The prior verse teaches us to *"seek first the kingdom of God and his righteousness."* Take time today to gather your family around the living room and spend time enjoying each other. Open the Bible as a family and read it together. Pray together. Do something fun. The fun does not have to be expensive or costly. Fun to a kid is just spending time with them. It could be a puzzle or board game. Maybe it is playing a video game with them and just hanging out. Maybe it is going to the park or walking along a nature trail. The point is, when I find myself focused on things that overwhelm me, what brings me back is when I divert my anxious focus to the blessings that are right in front of me and enjoy the moment I have today. You know what is right for your family. You know how these verses should be applied to your life. Today is not the end, but maybe the beginning of turning over your future into the hands of God. It is trusting that He knows what you need. It is trusting that He desires to have a relationship with you. You have learned how to talk with Him. You have learned how to not trust the things the world says to trust in. Now, we just have to live it.

In James 1:22-25, we read, *"But be doers of the word, and not hearers only, deceiving yourselves. For if anyone is a hearer of the word and not a doer, he is like a man who looks intently at his natural face in a mirror. For he looks at himself and goes away and at once forgets what he was like. But the one who looks into the perfect law, the law of liberty, and perseveres, being no hearer who forgets but a doer who acts, he will be blessed in his doing."* I love this passage because it takes away the excuses of tomorrow and says do it today. Make today the day that you take action. All these devotions and Bible studies are not just to give you knowledge, but they are meant to move you to action. It is putting the Scripture into practice and living it out. There is no better time than right now. I love how Paul words it when it comes to our relationship with Jesus. In 2 Corinthians 6:1-2, he writes, *"Working together with him, then, we appeal to you not to receive the grace of God in vain. For he says, 'In a favorable time I listened to you, and in a day of salvation I have helped you.' Behold, now is the favorable time; behold, now is the day of salvation."*

I pray these devotions are of value to you. I pray they help you know God better. My ultimate desire is that, through these last few weeks, you are able to see that the promises of God are 100% trustworthy. Despite the way we think sometimes, God promises us His grace and salvation today! Trust in His promises and know that He is true and trustworthy. Live it out and let tomorrow come with its own struggles. Today, this moment, and this time is what you have. What are you going to do with it? Be blessed!

OUR MISSION

Matthew 28:19-20: *"Go therefore and make disciples of all nations, baptizing them in the name of the Father and of the Son and of the Holy Spirit, teaching them to observe all that I have commanded you. And behold, I am with you always, to the end of the age."*

REACH

At The River Church, you will often hear the phrase, "We don't go to church, we are the Church." We believe that as God's people, our primary purpose and goal is to go out and make disciples of Jesus Christ. We encourage you to reach the world in your local communities.

GATHER

Weekend Gatherings at The River Church are all about Jesus, through singing, giving, serving, baptizing, taking the Lord's Supper, and participating in messages that are all about Jesus and bringing glory to Him. We know that when followers of Christ gather together in unity, it's not only a refresher it's bringing life-change.

GROW

Our Growth Communities are designed to mirror the early church in Acts as having *"all things in common."* They are smaller collections of believers who spend time together studying the Word, knowing and caring for one another relationally, and learning to increase their commitment to Christ by holding one another accountable.

The River Church
8393 E. Holly Rd.
Holly, MI 48442

theriverchurch.cc • info@theriverchurch.cc

Made in the USA
Monee, IL
03 August 2023

40279898R00168